A Pastor's Wife:

Conversations with Wives of Men in Ministry

A Pastor's Wife:

Conversations with Wives of Men in Ministry

K. M. Mamane, C. Z. Mambi,
F. O. Mpunzana, S. M. Nyawo, C. P. Xaba

Edited by Susan Binion

UBI Publishing
Hilton, South Afrixa

2011

Copyright © 2011 by UBI Publishing
Union Bible Institute
P.O. Box 50
Hilton 3245
South Africa

Tel: 27 33 343 4547
Fax: 27 33 343 1975
E-mail: lit@ubi-edu.co.za
Internet: www.ubi-edu.co.za

UBI Publishing is a non-profit publishing enterprise of the Union Bible Institute. UBI Publishing exists to serve Union Bible Institute and the churches of southern Africa by providing materials to encourage believers' devotion to Christ, commitment to biblical truth, and ability to minister in a changing world.

ISBN: 978-0-9584182-4-9

Unless otherwise noted, Scripture quotations are from the
HOLY BIBLE, NEW INTERNATIONAL VERSION. Copyright © 1973, 1978, 1984 by International Bible Society. Used by permission of Zondervan Publishing House.

Other Scripture quotations are taken from the following sources:
Scripture quotations marked (NKJV) are from the New King James Version. Copyright © 1982 by Thomas Nelson, Inc. Used by permission. All rights reserved.

Scripture quotations marked (NASB) are from the NEW AMERICAN STANDARD BIBLE®, Copyright © 1960,1962,1963,1968,1971,1972,1973,1975,1977,1995 by The Lockman Foundation. Used by permission.

Scripture quotations marked (CEV) are from the Contemporary English Version Copyright © 1991, 1992, 1995 by American Bible Society. Used by permission.

Scripture quotations taken from the Amplified® Bible, Copyright © 1954, 1958, 1962, 1964, 1965, 1987 by The Lockman Foundation. Used by permission. (www.Lockman.org)

Cover Design & typesetting: Lou Levine, Stylish Impressions, Pietermaritzburg.

Printed by Intrepid Printers (Pty) Ltd - 5323

Cover Photographs by Wes Spradley, Marie Bjorklund, and Andrew Sisson
Contributor page photographs (pp142-144) by Susan Binion, Thomas Hasenknopf & Andrew Sisson. Diagram page 39 by Jennie Strycker.

Contents

Foreword		vii
	Mukololo Dr Takalani Dube	
Introduction		ix
	Susan Binion	
Acknowledgements		xi
Chapter 1	A Pastor's Wife: Who is She?	1
	Clare Zasembo Mambi	
Chapter 2	Handling Expectations	9
	Clare Zasembo Mambi	
Chapter 3	His Call to Ministry – Mine as Well?	16
	Sonene M. Nyawo	
Chapter 4	God's Priorities for a Godly Woman	25
	Christine Phumelele Xaba	
Chapter 5	Marriage and Ministry	38
	Susan Binion	
Chapter 6	Children, Family Life and Ministry	48
	Christine Phumelele Xaba	
Chapter 7	Hospitality: Opening Our Hearts and Homes	55
	Christine Phumelele Xaba	
Chapter 8	Managing the Family Finances	62
	Fikile Octavia Mpunzana	
Chapter 9	Friendships Inside and Outside the Church	76
	Khumsa Myrtle Mamane	

Chapter 10	Conflict, Criticism and Forgiveness *Fikile Octavia Mpunzana*	84
Chapter 11	Basic Counselling Skills *Susan Binion*	100
Chapter 12	Widowhood and the Ministry *Khumsa Myrtle Mamane*	109
Chapter 13	Rest and Refreshment in Ministry *Susan Binion*	118
Chapter 14	Conclusion: The Ministry Received *Clare Zasembo Mambi*	125
Postscript	A Word from a Young Pastor's Wife	129
Appendix 1	Surviving Bible School *Khumsa Mamane and Susan Binion*	132
Appendix 2	Writing a Will	139
About the Authors		142
Endnotes		145

Foreword

I am very excited by this timely work that the pastors' wives set out to do! They are true sons (daughters) of Issachar, who understand the signs of the times. Pastors' wives have largely been ignored in Christian literature. This book therefore covers a very important topic for this day and age. It is written especially for the African continent but has global relevance.

I became a pastor's wife by default. As a teenager I prayed that I would get married to a pastor because I figured it was my guaranteed entrance to heaven! As I became older I began to understand my relationship with God. I knew that I did not need to be married to a pastor to have an eternal relationship with God, and that vision became erased from my plans.

I was not too surprised, though, when the teacher I fell in love with and was planning to get married to approached me one day and said, "I believe I am called." I began to understand that though my prayer as a teenager had been made out of selfishness, God had a plan and He had already been at work in me to prepare me for this assignment.

I have been a pastor's wife now for ten years, currently overseeing a large congregation with satellites. There were times I had no clue what was expected of me, times when I was rebellious to the expectations I sensed from the congregation and my husband, times when I felt like I was drowning and times when quitting would have been welcomed.

Through all this I have learnt that even though God prepares us, we also need to work with Him by availing ourselves of teachings. The pastors have their fraternals and networks developed in Bible schools, but their wives have no support system. This book creates that support.

The lessons have such wide application that they can be used for any woman's situation. I recommend its use for:

- Pastors—to better love, support and understand their wives
- Pastors' wives—to better understand their role and find love, healing and support
- Pastors' kids—to better understand their parents' calling and create conversation platforms and prayer items for the family
- The men's and women's ministries—for their own growth and to create empathy for the office of the first lady

- Anybody interested in the ministry and in marriage—the lessons are precious

Pastors' wives are children of God, church members, ministers of the gospel, committee members, children, siblings, wives and lovers, mothers to their biological children and mothers to the congregation, administrators, employees/employers/business owners—the list goes on and on! Sometimes it can be overwhelming.

A pastor's wife needs to understand each of these roles and plan her life in such a way that she is able to execute all excellently. I read a quotation once that says: "We do not all need to be great, but we all need to do things with great love and excellence." Perhaps as far as earthly greatness is concerned, a pastor's wife may never become "great". But if all she focuses on is doing things with great grace, love and excellence, she shall have done greatly!

Marriage is the only school where people get their certificates before they write their examinations. As a pastor's wife, you get double certificates without undergoing any training. In order to pass the examinations that follow (the tests, trials and tribulations of marriage and the ministry) this book will be of much help.

Read this book three times: the first time straight through as a novel, the second time as a devotional guide, and the third time gather some women around yourself and read it together in a fellowship.

Thank you to the authors for such wonderful insights, wisdom and love!

I salute you and the work the LORD entrusted to you women of virtue. May this grow...

Mukololo Dr Takalani Dube

Mother of Nations
Director: Ethekwini Community Church
Founding President: Centre of HOPE

Introduction

Susan Binion

Editor

Over ten years ago, the women on staff at the Union Bible Institute saw a need to reach out to the wives of the married men who came to study for the ministry. Many of these wives were unable to accompany their husbands to Bible college. While their husbands were learning to expound the Scriptures, the wives were passing tests of a different sort—tending farms, holding down jobs as nurses or teachers, being both father and mother to their children, managing crises alone. These sacrifices stretched their faith, but left them in the dark about what their husbands had experienced for three years at Bible school.

So the ministry of *Sisebenza Kanyekanye* was born, a ministry whose purpose was to encourage wives of students and prepare them for their unique role as wives of men in ministry. We also found that wives of alumni, as they returned to campus and shared their stories, had met with some discouragements along the way. We searched for a culturally relevant book to use as we met with these women but found nothing that was exactly what we needed.

UBI Publishing agreed to publish a book that would not only give direction and hope to future pastors' wives, but also encourage the many others who were already serving in that role. A team of experienced pastors' wives from several different church affiliations was called together to write chapters on topics that were closest to their hearts. Many other pastors' wives shared their heartaches and joys with us. As we met together, it was clear we shared a passion for the wives of men in ministry.

This book is written for women whose husbands are involved in ministry, whether full-time or part- time. But any woman who wants to serve the Lord will find treasures of wisdom in its pages. Our heart's desire is for the women who read this book to feel competent and confident in the work of the Lord and to know the blessings of being a pastor's wife. Not every pastor's wife will herself be involved full time in ministry but she will share her husband's call as she supports him from her heart. We hope that as we share God's faithfulness through stories from our own lives and the lives of others, and as we look into God's Word, the readers will grow in their faith and begin to see God's power at work in their own lives.

We are grateful for the pastors' wives who have shared their stories with us. Their testimonies are what make the chapters relevant and meaningful. In most cases we have changed the names and details of the people involved to preserve their privacy.

There are questions at the end of every chapter which can be used for personal reflection or discussion. Our hope is that you will gather with other pastors' wives and go through the book together. As you discuss the questions, share your own stories, and pray for one another, we trust you will be encouraged in your role as a pastor's wife.

It has been a privilege to serve as the coordinator of the group of women who have met together to write this book. We have passionately discussed and passionately prayed about the contents of this book. May you be blessed as you discover your unique calling as the wife of a man in ministry.

Acknowledgements

We are grateful to all of the pastors' wives who have shared their stories with us so freely. Their contributions to this project have given life and heart to the book.

For many years in our *Sisebenza Kanyekanye* ministry at UBI we used Leah Marasigan Darwin's book, *Yes! I'm a Pastor's Wife!* to encourage the student wives. Her book served as the model for this book as we began to decide which topics and principles should be included. Thank you, Leah, for your encouragement over the years, and for your continued input into the lives of pastors' wives all over the world. The discussion questions found at the end of Chapters 3, 4, 5 and 8 are adapted from questions Susan Binion wrote for the second edition of Leah's book.

The biblical principles presented in Chapter 10, "Conflict, Criticism, and Forgiveness," are based on Ken Sande's excellent book, *The Peacemaker*, © 1991, 1997, 2004 by Kenneth Sande, Baker books, a division of Baker Publishing Group. We are grateful for permission to use this material.

A special thanks to LeAnne Hardy, free-lance editor and author of *Beads and Braids* (Shuter and Shooter), for her professional advice and polish. Her enthusiasm for the book kept us going when we might have given up.

We are grateful to our husbands who have supported us in this project in many ways—from typing to transportation to editorial suggestions—but more importantly with their love, encouraging words and confidence in us.

Most of all, we thank God for walking with us and guiding us throughout this project. When we would hit snags or delays, we could sense His leading and encouragement. He who called us is faithful, and He has done it. Thank you, Jesus.

> I knew my husband had a call on his life, but I never fathomed the magnitude of it all.

> Nothing in my prior life prepared me for the road ahead—that of being a pastor's wife.

Chapter 1

A Pastor's Wife: Who is She?

Clare Zasembo Mambi

One day you wake up and discover that you are going to be a pastor's wife. You may wonder whether you will be good enough to help in your husband's calling. Will you mope around at home while he is busy doing God's work, or will you be preaching evangelistic tent crusades? Perhaps you never really thought you would be married to a pastor. Perhaps you were already busy with your own ministry before you married. For some the call to pastoral ministry comes after they have been married for some time and working a secular job. Others marry someone who is already a pastor. Maybe since your childhood you have dreamt of having a millionaire for a husband. What you may not realise—and what we hope you will come to see as you read this book—is that as a pastor's wife, you have won a millionaire in the kingdom of God. You will have the joy of sharing in those kingdom riches.

Whether you are called a pastor's wife, a ministry wife, or "first lady", as the wife of a man in ministry, you are a woman who has been honoured by God. You are in a position of great influence, both with your husband and with the congregation. In Proverbs 31 we hear the words of a man who knows the power of the woman in his life. He has only words of praise for her. Here are some of the important points he raises:

- She is of noble character.
- She is worth more than rubies.
- Her husband has full confidence in her.
- She brings him good and no harm.
- She is diligent.
- She uses her tongue well.
- She is a good house manager.
- She is a blessing to her children.
- Her husband is full of praises for her.
- She fears the Lord.

As a ministry wife, you will have the opportunity to develop into a woman of noble character as you serve beside your husband. Praise God for ministry wives! Be assured that you have great potential. Remember that as a woman, you are the crowning glory of God's creation.

In the Bible, we see many women who had noble character and demonstrated much power for good in the lives of their families and communities.

- ❖ **Moses' mother** was brave and did not fear the command of the king. This bravery was the product of her faith. In her strong faith she knew that the living God of Israel would save her son (Exodus 2:1-2).

- ❖ **Miriam**, young as she was, had strong faith too. She stood there waiting for someone to come and take Moses to safety. When the occasion presented itself she exercised her faith by asking Pharaoh's daughter to allow her to go and find a nurse for the baby (Exodus 2:4-7).

- ❖ **Shiphrah and Puah**, two midwives, expressed their fear of God by disobeying the wicked king's command and saving the baby boys (Exodus 1:15-21).

- ❖ **Hannah**, when she prayed for a child, did not make a selfish request. Instead, she demonstrated her faith in God by asking for a child who would be given back to the Lord as His servant (1 Samuel 1:9-28).

The Many Roles of a Pastor's Wife

In this book we are going to discuss the many roles a pastor's wife may fill. It is often difficult to know where to start. It is imperative that you begin by submitting yourself to the Lord by spending time studying the Scriptures and praying. It helps to have a healthy relationship with God. He is the one who knows you well. King David in one of his psalms says, "For you created my inmost being; ... your eyes saw my unformed body. All the days ordained for me were written in your book before one of them came to be" (Psalm 139:13, 16). Tell him about your fears, perplexities and anxieties, all that you think people expect from you, including your pastor husband. You will find God is a faithful friend.

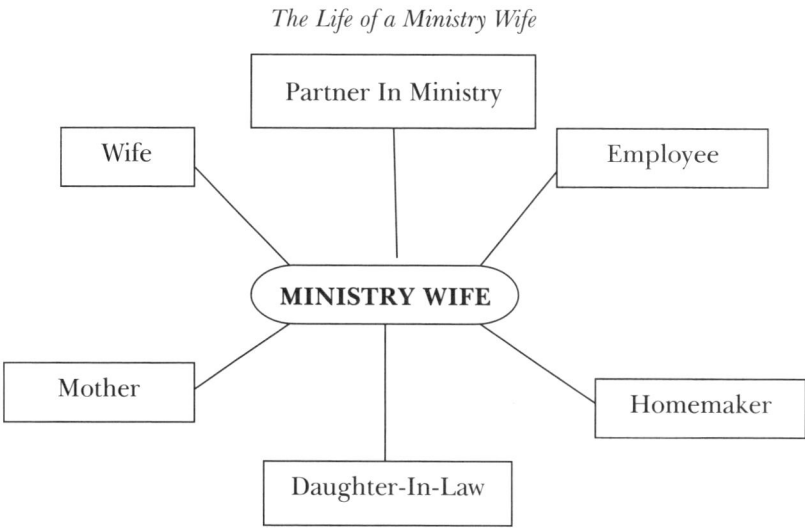

The Life of a Ministry Wife

You are first and foremost **wife to your husband.** When your husband proposed to you and you agreed to marry him, he asked you to marry a *man*, not "the pastor". You became husband and wife. You were interested in him as your husband. If his call to ministry came after you were married, you likely had to make some adjustments. But remember that your relationship takes top priority. If it is unhealthy, the ministry will suffer. On the other hand, if you have a healthy marriage relationship you will be able to work together harmoniously, encouraging each other. In Ecclesiastes 4:9, 10 we read: "Two are better than one, because they have a good return for their work: if one falls down, his friend can help him up. But pity the man who falls and has no one to help him up!"

As a **mother** you take care of your children. This in itself is no easy task. Parenting can be demanding. God through Moses required Israelite parents to teach the Word diligently to their children. He said parents must talk to their children about God's Word "when you sit at home, and when you walk along the road, when you lie down and when you get up" (Deuteronomy 6:6-7). This is what God also requires us to do in our parenting. Even if you have done all that you believe needs to be done, there is no guarantee that your children will all obey the gospel. Some may be wayward. This can cause much pain and impact the work you are doing.

It is also a reality of life that you are a **daughter-in-law** to your husband's parents. You may not always have enough time to visit your husband's family. Sometimes you miss family gatherings which may clash with the tight schedule of the church. You also have parents of your own. Loving both sets of parents equally can be a good testimony to others and an encouragement to your husband. Show them the love that is due to them, in the Lord.

A ministry wife is also a **homemaker**. When Paul speaks of wives being homemakers in Titus 2:5, he is highlighting the non-negotiable responsibility of a Christian wife to keep the home for her husband and children. The importance of good house management is again mentioned in 1 Timothy 5:14. This helps have a happy atmosphere in your house, an atmosphere that is conducive to hospitality.

In some cases, the ministry wife is an **employee** in a secular job. There is much pressure from working two "jobs", that of a pastor's wife and employment outside the home. You will find that you have many responsibilities to balance all at once. You will have to be organised and know God's priorities for your life each day. It may happen that you miss church meetings and conferences because of your work schedule. But there are some advantages to working outside home. First, you can identify with the working women in your congregation. You may also be able to give generously to needy people and thus set a good example of giving. You can contribute to your family finances. For example, when I was employed as a teacher I was able to contribute towards the building of our home which has been a great blessing for the family as well as a centre of ministry for home groups and other church meetings.

One difficulty that may arise if you are employed is the possibility that your husband could be transferred to another local church and you may not be able to find a job in the new place immediately. As a result the family will be separated. This is fertile ground for temptations for both of you. If you have children they will live with one parent. The relationship can be tested with lack of mutual trust, financial constraints, and loneliness. It is said, "Half a loaf is better than no bread." Staying together with your husband is the best. If possible go with him wherever he is sent. You may not have all that you need, but God will always be in control. We do not obey God so that we can have it our way, but because He is God.

Being involved in these normal wife's responsibilities does not absolve the ministry wife from that all-important responsibility, namely, to be her pastor husband's **partner in ministry**. This is your call to serve with him in his ministry. In order to serve freely you need to exercise your ministry where your spiritual gifts and natural talents fit, according to the abilities God gave you. If you are employed or have small children, you may not be able to share in everything. But he must know that you are with him in your heart. As one young pastor's wife put it, "I was determined to give my husband my undivided moral and spiritual support." That is what your husband needs most of all, and it is what only *you* can give.

Seasons of our Life

As you try to balance all the roles you fill as a ministry wife, it will help to be aware of the seasons of a woman's life. There is a time for everything (Ecclesiastes 3:1). Leah Marasigan Darwin in her book, *Yes! I'm a Pastor's Wife!*, talks about these seasons.[1]

- **Childhood**—from birth until the age of puberty.
- **Young womanhood**—when we turned teenagers with all the hormonal changes we went through.

- **Married without kids**—first few years of our lives as young women with no kids to care for yet.
- **Married with small kids**—right before the children go to school.
- **Married with schooling kids**—we have more time on our hands to go to minister.
- **Empty nest**—when our kids are grown, have left the house and have families of their own.

The seasons of your life may not look exactly like these. For example, in the third season, "married without kids", some people wait for a few years before having children, but others start their family right away. It depends on each couple's plans and God's sovereignty. Most people experience the empty nest, but others find grandchildren staying with them due to unforeseen circumstances. Those that experience grandchildren living with them should regard that as a divine opportunity and raise those children to the glory of God. Remember that both Lois and Eunice influenced Timothy.

It is the God of seasons who created all the phases we go through. You need to ask for His guidance and blessings as you go through them. Understand that there is a purpose for each one. Some allow more free time than others. Enjoy them all, and you will be able to look back and give thanks to God for the lessons you learnt, simple or hard. For example, when you have small children you may not be very involved in ministry outside your home. If you were involved in ministry as a single woman, you may miss the work you used to do and feel that you are no longer useful to the Lord. Accept the phases in your life, and help your pastor husband and the church people to understand which phase you are going through by communicating it clearly. This will help you avoid frustration.

Be Encouraged

In Matthew 6:33 we are told to seek first the kingdom of God and His righteousness and all the other things we need will be added to us. We are urged to tell all to Him who says, "In all your ways acknowledge Him, and He shall direct your paths" (Proverbs 3:6, NKJV). You must also know that He has regard for those who are humble at heart. Be assured that God is looking for people whom the world calls foolish and weak, poor and insignificant. As you have come to serve Him, you can adopt A. W. Tozer's words: "You [God] are quick to mark every simple effort to please you, and just to overlook imperfections when I meant to do your will."[2] God is delighted with all the good deeds you do in His name, big or small. As He is a potter, He is able to mould you over and over again if you keep submitting yourself to Him. In 2 Corinthians 4:7 the apostle Paul speaks about the treasure that is contained in earthen vessels, which means that every victory and every accomplishment come from God. They are not from our strength or wisdom.

You may be going through a hard time, not knowing where the next meal will come from. Many wives share the story of their pastor husband not having a salary for months. In some cases, this situation happens because the pastor may have a disagreement with influential members of the congregation. They make sure they keep him under control by not giving their tithe. In other cases, the church may be too poor to pay the pastor's salary, or it may be that the pastor is church planting.

When you go through such experiences be assured that God will intervene in one way or another. Our experience is a case in point. When we were church planting at Edendale we were struggling along with the small support we received from some Christian brothers and sisters. More than 50% of the money was used for rent. We had to pay school fees for our children, transport and food for our family of five. I was also pregnant at this time. Two of the children needed registration money for their Matric exams. They had been sent back home by the school to fetch the registration fees.

One Wednesday morning one of the children came to fetch the money. I told her to go to their teacher and tell her that I was going to pay the money on Friday. On the same day, after she had left for school, I was praying as I usually did at noon. While I was still praying I heard a car parking outside followed by a knock at the door. I prepared to meet the visitor by wiping the tears from my face.

To my amazement there was an elderly lady I knew well. She asked me to accompany her to the car. It was full of groceries! She also left us some money--enough to pay the registration fees for the children. This lady had no prior knowledge of our situation. We paid the money to the school--a day earlier than promised.

God intervened by touching someone who knew nothing about our problem to provide for our family. He indeed is our faithful Provider.

You may feel like quitting the race before you start. Be encouraged. God understands and will give you strength, as He has promised in 2 Corinthians 12:9-10: "My power is made perfect in weakness." Paul could only respond, "When I am weak, then I am strong." It is this same Lord who said, "Never will I leave you; never will I forsake you (Hebrews 13:5).

Above all, nothing can be as encouraging as seeing people come to the Lord and growing in the faith. As ministers of the gospel, God also provides us with many people who pray for us and contribute towards the Lord's work and the needs of the family. What can be more satisfying than to know that you are in the will of God and that He will reward you for what you are doing?

Questions to think about and discuss:

1. As you begin this book, what are the questions you hope will be answered about being a pastor's wife?
2. What are some of the fears you may have about being a pastor's wife?
3. Which of the roles of a pastor's wife do you find most challenging? Which are easiest for you?
4. Which phase of life are you in right now? How does it affect your ability to fulfil your role as a pastor's wife?
5. What do you think some of the blessings of being a pastor's wife might be?

Chapter 2

Handling Expectations

Clare Zasembo Mambi

So many times you hear remarks like these from the wives of pastors who used to have secular jobs, as well as from those who married men already in ministry. You must always remember that in ministry you will have big surprises, and of course God hides the future from us. We might not stand if we knew what was going to happen the next day.

Expectations come from many different sources. We have expectations that we place on ourselves, creating a heavy burden. We hope to be super-ministry wives, which is the number one method of frustrating oneself. We must let God work through us and be ever willing to learn and experience new things.

Congregations also have expectations of the pastor's wife. They may expect her to teach Sunday school and be on its leadership committee whether she is gifted and trained in teaching or not. She must be able to lead praise and worship. She is also expected to lead and teach the ladies' meetings and have an outgoing personality. It is true that when you and your pastor husband are still planting a church, you cannot escape doing most of these duties until there are members who will fit in. Ephesians 4:11-13 tells us that the job of the pastor is to *equip* the congregation for ministry, not to do it all himself. So you also can help train others and allow them to use their gifts.

One ministry wife found it difficult to change her dress code. She had been working for some years in a secular job with her husband before they went to ministry. She had to quit her job and join her husband in full-time ministry. She found it very difficult to dress formally. It is true many of us like to wear casual clothes, but there are places where we need to dress more formally to be presentable.

Another wife testified about a situation where she and her husband had to leap from the casual wardrobe they were accustomed to into formal wear. She says, "We had to align what we put on with the new status we had been ushered to by popular demand. There were times we had to spend money we did not have so that we may appear confident in public, especially in church or weddings we are invited to with the senior pastor of the church."

It was in a general church conference where a pastor's family was told they were to leave a parish where they had served for nine years. They had lived in a manse for all those years since they graduated from college. When they first came to the parish they were provided with furniture and everything they needed for the house. When they left they had to leave everything there. To their amazement when they arrived at the new parish they were given an empty house. No one ever told them they would need their own furniture. Fortunately, God in His grace provided them with their daily needs.

When Jesus taught His disciples how to pray, He said, "Give us each day our daily bread" (Luke 11:3). This was a lesson they had to learn—to depend on God for their daily needs. Paul in Philippians 4:11-12 says: "I am not saying this because I am in need, for I have learned to be content whatever the circumstances." Paul could say, "I am content." Even though he was in prison his general attitude about life and his God was one of contentment. He carried it in his heart wherever he went. This is the attitude we are to adopt in this calling.

There are some expectations from our congregations which may not be reasonable. One lady was hurt so deeply she once said,

"If I had known, I would not have married my husband." In her situation she married a pastor whose first wife had passed away. When the ladies from a sister congregation came to welcome her, one of them said they would not accept her unless she would be like the first wife. She first thought it was a slip of the tongue. But the phrase was repeated until it wounded her heart. When it was time for her to reply she could not talk properly because she was in tears. She told them how difficult it was to fit into someone else's shoes. She added that her intention was to be like Jesus. After some time the congregation changed their hearts and accepted her for who she was.

When Things are Difficult

In situations where everything seems to go wrong you can choose to be cheerful and everything will seem right. "The cheerful heart has a continual feast" (Proverbs 15:15). There will be gloomy days because we are still in this fallen world. But there is a difference between temporary and permanent gloom. We must be careful what we portray when we encounter negative situations because it is often contagious. Happiness is just as catching as gloom. In Proverbs 17:22 we read, "A cheerful heart is good medicine, but a crushed spirit dries up the bones." The God of all comfort will comfort us in all our tribulation. Remember how Jesus spoke to Mary directly and personally from the cross. Jesus noticed her, cared for her, and she was comforted (John 19:26-27).

It is impossible to satisfy everybody. Do not try to imitate someone else. What you do, do with the ability God has given you and use the gifts that God has given you and you will serve with freedom and love (Matthew 25:15b). If you have to outdo anyone it must be you. People in all ages have experienced difficult situations like we often do. Dr Larry Crabb has said,

> Faith is required because life can be overwhelmingly confusing. Hope for a better day is all we can cling to in those honest moments of facing life's disappointments. And love is the only approach to life that achieves God's purposes and gives us a sense of relationship with Christ and others.[1]

So be careful of your attitude. If you tend to say, "I don't care what people say or think of me," it would help to look and see if that attitude portrays the love of Christ the way Larry Crabb has described it. Should you feel that that attitude comes from a heart desperate for help, it would be advisable to ask for counsel from others as we are told to "encourage one another and build each other up" (1 Thessalonians 5:11). We must realise the privilege we have to be part of God's family here on earth.

How Should I Handle Expectations?

Remember that God is your Master.

Put Him first and please Him above all. Then you may find that people will also be happy with what you do (Colossians 3:23). Do not worry that you do not have as many gifts as other people. The yardstick that God uses to measure you is faithfulness—unequal gifts but equal faithfulness. Remember what Jesus went through when He was on earth. Consider also the ladies who suffer in the persecuted countries. This can make us count our hurts as the "momentary light afflictions" the apostle Paul speaks about in 2 Corinthians 4:17. We must strive to grow in the love and the knowledge of God, knowing that there are no wasted experiences for a believer.

Know God's purposes for your life.

God has His own purposes and I believe He expects each one of His children to follow those purposes. To accomplish His purposes He uses people in the church as He pleases. Jesus clearly understood His life purpose and made it very clear when He was under trial by Pontius Pilate: "For this reason I was born, and for this I came into the world, to testify to the truth" (John 18:37). John elsewhere reiterates this truth when he says: "The reason the Son of God appeared was to destroy the devil's work" (1 John 3:8). Our purpose should be in line with God's overall purposes. You need to ask yourself the questions, "What is the purpose of my life? Why do I get out of bed every morning? Why did God save me in the first place? Why did he give me a pastor for a husband?" A strong sense of purpose and meaning rooted in God and His purpose will help you do your work faithfully.

Know and use your gifts.

When you accept Jesus as your Lord you are given gifts of the Holy Spirit (Ephesians 4:7). You should never doubt that you are gifted. You also have your natural talents and abilities. 1 Corinthians 6:20 says, "God paid a great price for you. So use your body to honour God" (CEV). We serve Him because we owe Him our life. When Jesus healed Peter's mother-in-law, she instantly stood up and served Him (Matthew 8:15).

Some people will argue that they do not know their gifts. One way to discover your gifts is to start doing something to serve others. Understanding your gifts will help discern God's purpose for your life. Christ is the equipper. He equips you with the knowledge of Himself and His Word, with the purpose of building your character so that you may be like Him. Christ will equip you for the job you are called for as a ministry wife.

In Romans 12:1-2, before teaching about the gifts of the Spirit, the apostle Paul says, "Be transformed." Without transformation you cannot be effective in the Lord's work however gifted you may be. In Romans 12:3-8 some spiritual gifts are listed:

- Prophecy—speaking the truth, not necessarily predicting the future[3]
- Ministry—serving and helping
- Teaching—ability to interpret and explain God's word
- Exhortation—encouraging, comforting and strengthening believers
- Giving—sharing with others to glorify God
- Leading—influencing others, doing administration
- Showing mercy—offering sympathy, sensitivity and practical help to those in suffering and sorrow

In 1 Peter 4:11 the apostle urges the believers to use their gifts, saying: "If anyone speaks, he should do it as one speaking the very words of God. If anyone serves, he should do it with the strength God provides...."

Ministry wife, you are called like all other believers to work for the Lord. Not putting your gift into use deprives the church of the goodness that the Lord bestowed on the church and the world through you. Will you start using your gifts to the fullest and be blessed while you are a blessing? Remember, these are spiritual gifts, so let the Spirit do the work in you and through you.

Realise that you are still growing in Christ.

You must understand that God is not yet finished with you. Know whom you serve, and do whatever you do as if for Him. There are many expectations that I have not discussed or mentioned here. You may be faced with one or more of them. Be of good courage, and know that your failures and mistakes are part of all the things in which "God works for the good of those who love Him, who have been called according to His purpose" (Romans 8:28). The stresses, hostilities and feelings of anxiety that you experience will make you depend on God, who said in His Word we must trust Him with all our hearts and depend on His adequacy. The first couple of years will be an adjustment as you learn to understand people and their behaviour. God's love helps in that situation to adjust and be contented. Your ministry will be effective when you surrender your inadequacy to Him and let Him deal with your whole being.

Love Above All

A group of experienced pastors' wives were asked, "What do we do when the people of congregation love my husband, but they don't love me?" Their answer was simple: love them—love them anyway. Just love them." In Matthew 9:36 we are told: "When He saw the crowds, He had compassion on them, because they were harassed and helpless, like sheep without a shepherd." Jesus saw their need to be taught, cared for and loved. If this is how our Lord felt for people it follows that we, His servants, should do likewise. As you show compassion to people you work with, you will be showing signs of becoming more like Jesus. As you submit to Christ, He will make you a blessing. He will give you the power to overcome hard times and fulfil the calling he has given you.

Questions to think about and discuss:

1. What are some of the expectations your church or denomination places on ministry wives? How do you feel about these expectations?
2. What are some expectations you may have of yourself?
3. Does your husband have expectations of you in your role as a pastor's wife? How do you feel about them?
4. How do Proverbs 29:25 and Colossians 3:23-24 help you as you face the expectations of others?
5. Look at Ephesians 4:13-16. List as many purposes for spiritual gifts as you can find in the passage.
6. What do you think are the main gifts you bring to your role as a pastor's wife?
7. In what ways do you think you have grown since you became a pastor's wife?

> **MRS V**
> I married a pastor, and that is his calling, not mine. I draw boundaries between his call and my life.

> **MRS D**
> I married an electrician, but the Lord called him into ministry. I give him all my support.

> **MRS Z**
> My life as a pastor's wife is too hectic. I try to fit myself into this busy schedule, but I fail. I have now resolved to live my own life.

> **MRS T**
> I am not a pastor, but I enjoy supporting my husband's calling because I believe that God brought us together for a purpose.

Chapter 3

His Call to Ministry – Mine as Well?

Sonene M. Nyawo

The above speech bubbles are representative of the perceptions of various pastors' wives about their responsibilities as partners to the men of God in the ministry. There are those pastors' wives (like Mrs D and Mrs T), who have shown some high degree of dedication to the ideals of their husband's calling, and they have served alongside their husbands as supportive and reliable partners. Conversely, there are those (like Mrs V and Mrs Z) who have drawn boundaries between their husbands' calling and their own lives. They fail to realize they are yoked together with their husbands as a team to fulfil God's purpose on earth through their service.

Surprisingly, the Bible does not issue any specific injunctions to pastors' wives, except in the passages whereby responsibilities for all wives are addressed. All wives, for example, are obliged to support and be submissive to their husbands (Ephesians 5:22-24). However, if God calls a man into His ministry, He calls the whole man, and that includes the wife and his entire family. St Paul (1Timothy 3:4) specifies the qualifications of a pastor and that his success will be determined by the love, support and respect that he receives from his submissive wife.

Amazingly, there is no training institution for girls who aspire to be pastors' wives. One is handpicked by God, and without any preparation she finds herself in this "deep end." It is not easy to be a pastor's wife, whether you felt the call on your life before marriage, or you just happened to marry someone in the ministry. When you experience some valleys in your life, and you find yourself at your lowest ebb, you then confront God with questions on His purposes and plans for your life. There are moments or even days in which a pastor's wife feels she can readily and willingly trade her position for something else, or even anything else. But you should draw some strength from the assurance that God has placed you in your unique situation for a unique purpose. He knows when you sit and when you rise; He perceives your thoughts from afar; He discerns your going out and your lying down; He is familiar with all your ways (Psalm 139:2-3).

The Pastor's Wife as a Helper

Every Christian woman, whether she is in the ministry or not, draws her inspiration to help her husband with his responsibilities, his tasks, his roles, his work and his calling from Genesis 2:18b, which says; "...I will make him a helper meet (suitable, adapted, completing) for him" (The Amplified Bible).

The Bible describes the creation of a woman with the word *made*, not *formed*, from dust. That gives the impression that God planned and supervised this "building" of the woman with the purpose that she would be a "helper suitable to a man." God Himself performed the first "major procedure" as medical experts would call it, and operated on Adam to *make* a woman.

The Hebrew word translated "helper" is *ezer*, which occurs 21 times in the Old Testament. In 2 instances in Genesis, *ezer* refers to the woman Eve. In 16 of the other 19 instances the word is used to describe God Himself. Obviously, the term cannot be said to represent some sort of subservient role. "Helper" is a term of function rather than worth. To be more precise, a pastor's wife does not lose value as a person by humbly assuming the role of a helper to her husband. She has the assignment of being helper in her home, family, community, and church. How does God help His people? By protecting, supporting, shielding, sustaining, delivering, comforting, giving hope, and blessing them. Likewise, the pastor's wife as a helper is supposed to protect, support, shield, sustain, deliver, comfort, give hope and bless all those she interacts with, either intimately or casually.

However, the term "helper" does not imply a hierarchy in the home or church; the woman is not the "master's slave" or second in command. The King's James Version uses the words *a help meet* rather than a *helper suitable*. The Amplified Bible uses the words, *a helper meet*. What is a *help meet/helper meet*? Webster's Ninth New Collegiate Dictionary defines *help* as "to give assistance or support to." The same dictionary gives the definition of the word *meet* as; "precisely adapted to a particular situation, need, or circumstance." A "help meet" therefore, is *one who is to give assistance or support and is precisely adapted (made to fit) to a particular situation, need or circumstance.* A help meet is precisely made—we might even say "wired"—to give assistance and support to the man God has made her for, her family, her church, and everyone she comes into contact with.

I wish all pastors wives would realise that God gave them to this world as a blessing to help men of God carry out their visions, and without them, the men of God are incomplete. If you have a lingering frustration with being created to be a helper, or if you still believe that being a helper limits an effective usage of your gifts or it relegates you to a weaker role, look again at the Scripture references and consider how God Himself is our helper (Psalm 10:14; 54:4; 118:6, 7).

Responsibilities of a Pastor's Wife

A pastor's wife has awesome responsibilities which require her to have a "sixth sense" in order to strike a good balance in her tasks and duties as she fulfils God's purpose in the ministry. She may not necessarily share the pulpit with her pastor-husband, but they are yoked together in God's vineyard. As God's child she is also endowed with spiritual gifts which should bless and edify the church they are serving. Some ministry women have failed to recognize this truth, and they close themselves into boxes, or even claim to play a low profile because they want to keep their home fires burning. Others prefer to remain home whilst praying for their husbands at the peripheries.

Whilst all these responsibilities are of vital importance, we should remember that an active and outgoing pastor's wife is a valuable asset that brightens the day as she accomplishes God's purposes amongst the congregants. That said, the pastor's wife should not over load herself with too many tasks in the church; she would otherwise find it difficult to effectively fulfil her other responsibilities as the queen of the parsonage. There is no reason why she should be choir conductor, Sunday school teacher, keyboard player, counsellor and committee member all at once. In assuming many positions in the church she runs the risk of failing to strike a balance in her responsibilities.

As part of her high calling, the pastor's wife should make her husband's ministry easier and more effective. The pastor as a human being sometimes experiences down moments in his own life where everything seems to go wrong: the carefully and strenuously prepared sermons fail to reach the mark; the Sunday attendance falls below average; he is flooded with criticisms for this and that; his visions and efforts are thwarted. To whom should he turn for encouragement and support? None other than his wife, who should come to his rescue. She can provide her shoulder for him to cry on and exercise the faith that God has given her. One writes about Martin Luther's wife who found her husband looking exceptionally gloomy, and she remarked, "Martin, God is dead." He rebuked her, and she responded by saying, "But Martin, you act as though He were dead." Martin got the point and he faced up to his responsibilities again.

The ministry woman is called to be an alert partner. Some pastors, for example, may unknowingly develop mannerisms that are offensive to those who sit in the pew. His wife can draw his attention to this limitation before the situation worsens. She should be her husband's most faithful and constructive critic as well as his greatest encourager. She ought to choose the right time and share her thoughts with love and kindness, remembering to praise him when he succeeds in correcting the fault. This provides good opportunities for his personal improvement and growth in the ministry. A pastor's wife cannot effectively serve this role if:

- she has no interest in her husband's sermons.
- she is often outside church during the service.
- she is always engaged in other commitments.
- she is not a prayer partner.
- she is not a good listener.
- she does not carry a diary to note down her husband's preaching.

If she refrains from the above negative habits and performs all her responsibilities with honesty and ardour, God the Father who sees in secret will bestow unique blessings upon her.

Other than the role she plays as a helper to her husband, she also fulfils her calling through ministering to her own children, who sadly, are kids that grow up in a fishbowl. The "PK's" (Pastor's Kids) as they are often labelled and defined, experience some pressure from the church to exhibit certain commendable behaviour. They are expected to make some sacrifices, which any children of their age may fail to make: they need to smile to everyone that squeezes their cheeks; they must refrain from any behaviour that will reflect negatively on their mom and dad; they must come early to church, and be the last to leave; they must dress "modestly," as defined by the congregants.

As a pastor's wife you have the greatest challenge to foster a healthy development in your children in the midst of all these pressures. You need first and foremost to inculcate an inner strength in their lives to have the desire to sincerely honour and fear the Lord more than people. Your primary focus should be to teach them to grow up loving Christ. Also share with them the privileges of being a pastor's family, and the eternal spiritual rewards that God has promised to all that support His servant. Shelter them against unconstructive, unhealthy conversations that might pollute their minds or even cast doubts on the authenticity of your ministry. Your kids will have great confidence in you if you stay actively involved in their world, which encompasses their activities, interests, and most importantly, their future.

Sign Up to be on Board

> I can do all things through Christ who strengthens me. (Philippians 4:13, NKJV)

The responsibilities of a ministry woman are quite taxing; one cannot effectively juggle all that is on her plate without God's enabling grace. In my ministry of 21 years, I have made the above quoted verse my motto, and I have seen God providing me with strength even in tough circumstances. My motto has helped me to cope with the commonly experienced stressors in the ministry, which include:

- unwarranted expectations
- fatigue
- never off duty/perception that you have to be always on duty
- learning to relate and be in harmony with all the generations in the church
- constant exposure to people's problems and pain
- maintaining a good marriage
- doing voluntary work, which may not be recognized
- coping with the feeling of being an unsung hero
- "fish-bowl" experiences; being observed and scrutinized—your kids and husband, your body language, your dress code, your tidy house and your everything
- loneliness
- expressed and unexpressed criticism

In the midst of all these stressors your right perspective and positive attitude towards your ministry to your husband, your children and the church sustains you. The realisation that you "can do all things through Christ" helps you to maintain your poise, sweetness, composure and dignity, even in the midst of violent emotional storms that may rage around you. Be convinced that you are a ministry woman by divine purpose. You can petition God to pull you out of this awesome responsibility, but He will not until His purposes are accomplished through your life.

Be encouraged by this testimony from a young pastor's wife who did not marry a pastor at all, but had to jump into the wagon whilst it was moving. She now serves alongside her husband in the ministry, as a helper and partner.

============

Bless the name of the Lord who is forever faithful. I am a witness to Paul's words when he says God makes his strength perfect in our weaknesses. I have been weak too many times, perhaps at the verge of giving up, but the Lord would inject His divine potency on my feeble knees and sustain me. It has not been easy being a pastor's wife, and it's still daunting even now. It has been a journey crammed with thorns and hurdles, but praise God who has kept me still.

Not very long ago, my husband of four years was ordained a prophet of the church after serving as a deacon for almost a decade. That day was a major turning point in our lives...nothing has remained the same. Nothing in my prior life had prepared me for the road ahead—that of being a pastor's wife....

The eyes of the brethren are glued on me as to how I relate with them. I have since learnt that church folk are fragile and sensitive. Their attitude and perception towards me and the pastor pose a constant concern since one has to be careful to be in good rapport with them or else they might leave the church on my account. Moreover, they, too, have their expectations: to be hugged, shake their hands and have an encouraging word for them as well as showing up for every service and ultimately to be a mother to them all....

Everybody tells you their problems and expects you to speak life into their situations and release a prophetic word to sustain them....Another territory that has presented unforeseen challenges was presentation...It has always been my assignment to ensure that the pastor is presentable for the multiple services he renders for the church.

In all, I have seen the unrelenting presence and hand of the Lord in my life and marriage. There [have] been storms that threatened to capsize my determination.... Nonetheless, I have not seen the sceptre of the wicked resting in the land allotted for me (Psalms 125:3). Now I know what God can do to for me because of the mountains and the valleys he has pulled [me through] and is still pulling me through.

==================

Remember that there are many women out there whom God could have called, but He picked you. He has empowered you and gifted you through His Holy Spirit to excel in your ministry. Lastly, prayerfully assist your husband in evaluating the spiritual atmosphere of the Church. As a woman of God, He has given you intuition, which is the ability to discern the character and intent of others. Use that ability in your ministry for the glory of the Lord.

Questions to think about and discuss:

1. How and when did your husband first sense God's call to full-time ministry? How did you feel about his call?

2. How are the following verses relevant to a woman who is struggling with being a pastor's wife? 1 Peter 3:1, 7; Ephesians 5:22, 25, 28-29.

3. How does what you learned in this chapter about being a "helper meet" for your husband encourage you in your role as a pastor's wife?

4. What is one way you can show your husband this week that you are "on board", that is, fully supportive of his call to ministry?

5. If your heart is resisting being a pastor's wife, which of the following might be a root reason: financial concerns, fear of being neglected, feeling inadequate, unable to live up to expectations, concerns about children? Where in God's Word will you find help for each of these concerns? Write down and memorise the specific verses that apply to your situation.

Discussion questions from this chapter are adapted from *Yes! I'm a Pastor's Wife, 2nd edition*, by Leah Marasigan Darwin (Makati, Philippines: Church Strengthening Ministry, Inc., 2007).

Sources Consulted

Beardsley, L. and Spry, T., *The Fulfilled Woman* (California: Harvest House Publishers, 1975).

Darwin, L.M., *Yes! I'm a Pastor's Wife! 2nd edition* (Makati City, Philippines: Church Strengthening Ministry, Inc., 2007).

George, E., *A Woman's High Calling* (Eugene, Oregon: Harvest House Publishers, 2001).

Dougherty, S., *Called By His Side* (Victory Christian Center, 1987).

MacArthur, J., *Twelve Extraordinary Women* (Nashville: Nelson Books, 2005).

Tucker, R.A., *Private Lives of Pastor's Wives* (Nigeria: Bride of Christ International LTD, 1981).

> As a pastors' wife and working mother, I have so much to do. How can I balance everything and be sure I am doing what God wants me to?

> The people in the church expect me to know a lot about the Bible. It's my husband that went to Bible college—not me!

> Sometimes I feel that my children are getting in the way of the ministry God is calling me to.

Chapter 4

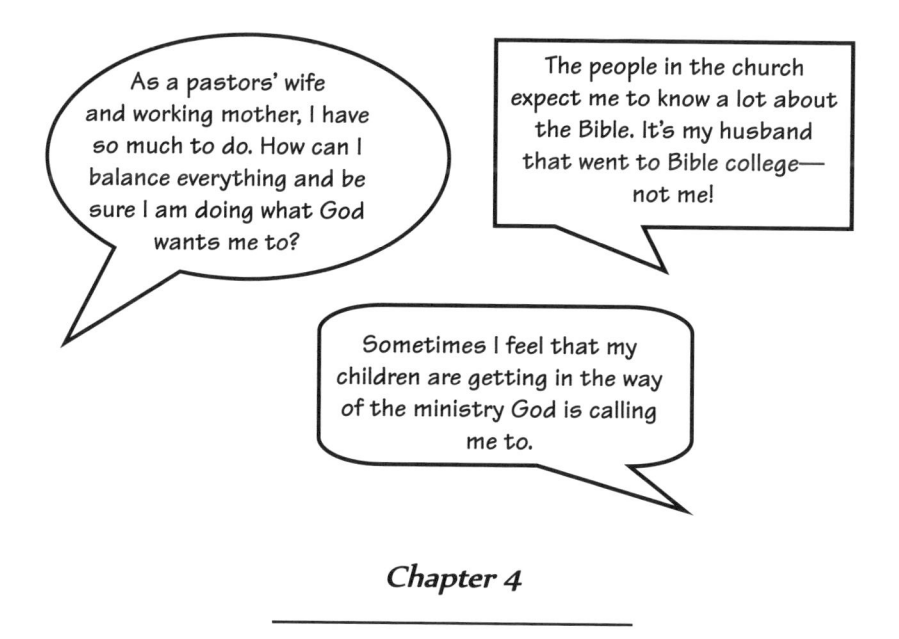

God's Priorities for a Godly Woman

Christine Phumelele Xaba

A young woman whose husband was training for ministry once asked, "What does it mean to be a pastors' wife? What is expected? What am I supposed to do?" You may be glad to hear that, for the most part, what you should do is no different than what any other committed Christian woman should do: seek God first and live to please Him in everything.

God uses very ordinary people to accomplish His plan. He once used a woman named Deborah to save Israel. Deborah was a homemaker just like many of the women in her day. She was also willing to serve God. God chose her to be a prophet and called her to do the work of a judge (Judges 4). Deborah called Barak to come and lead the armies to fight Sisera. Barak asked her to go with him. God used Deborah to conquer Sisera and his armies. Deborah did not boast in her accomplishment, but praised God (Judges 5). She also encouraged Barak to trust the Lord. Because of her obedience and faith, she had the privilege of being used by God to do great things for Him.

Would you like to be used by God like Deborah was? If so, you must begin with yourself—your own heart and life. God has biblical priorities for us as Christian women and pastors' wives.[1]

The First Step for a Godly Woman

Even though you are a pastor's wife, it is possible that you have never taken the first step to having a right relationship with God. The Bible calls this salvation—being born again. These are words we hear often. But what do they mean?

To understand what it means to be saved, we must first understand what the Bible says about our own hearts. All of us by nature choose to do things that make God sad, that break our relationship with him. The Bible calls this sin. Because God is holy and perfect, we must be perfect to have a relationship with Him. Our sin separates us from God. Another word for separation from God is death, both now and forever.

Our hearts turn the wrong way automatically, and need a total makeover from God. But because He loves us, God made a plan to bring us back to Him. 1 John 3:16 gives us the definition of love: "This is how we know what love is: Jesus Christ laid down his life for us." When Jesus died on the cross to pay the penalty for our sin, He opened the door to a new relationship with God. He didn't wait for us to become perfect. There is no way that we on our own can be good enough to save ourselves. "But God demonstrates his own love for us in this: while we were still sinners, Christ died for us." (Romans 5:8)

To start your friendship with God, first listen to God's Word, which has power to convict you of your sin. Then confess to Jesus that you are a sinner, and turn away from your sin. 1 John 1:9 says, "If we confess our sins, he is faithful and just and will forgive us our sins and purify us from all unrighteousness." Put your trust in Christ's death on the cross and His resurrection from the dead to pay the penalty for your sin. By doing this, you will receive a new heart that wants to follow God, and the power to do it through His Holy Spirit. You will be born again.

The Bible says, "If you confess with your mouth 'Jesus is Lord,' and believe in your heart that God raised him from the dead, you will be saved." (Romans 10:9-10) We read in John 9 that the man whose eyes were opened by Jesus said, "Lord, I believe," and he worshipped Jesus. If your spiritual eyes have been opened by Jesus and you have come to know who He is, will you too believe in Him and worship Him as your Lord and Saviour? Receive Him into your heart by faith and trust Him for your life—today.

By giving your life to Jesus, know that you have chosen something that will never be taken from you (Luke 10:38-42). All of us who have taken this first step with God have found that our lives have new purpose and power. We have found God faithful in every way. We know that you can trust and rely on God in every part of your life.

A Godly Woman Loves God Above All

It is also very important to have a heart that is wholly devoted to God. In Luke 10:38-42 we see Mary's devoted heart to the things of God. She saw it as very important to leave everything that she had been doing and spend time with Jesus. That shows that Mary loved God above everything else. A woman who loves God above all else will be able to say to Him, "Anything, anywhere, anytime, at any cost—I belong to you. Do as you wish with my life."

Women who have a deep love for God will show the whole world that this is so by the way they live. They must choose God's ways at every opportunity. Proverbs 3:6 teaches us that if we as godly women acknowledge Him in every way and every circumstance, God will direct our paths and lead us through every situation that we face. This means that before we take any action we must consult Him, trusting Him to give us the right words and attitudes at the right time.

As women who are born again, we have the Holy Spirit living in our hearts to lead and guide us. Psalm 32:8 promises us that God will instruct and teach us in the way we should go. He will also begin to change our character over time, making us more like Jesus as we yield our hearts to Him. He will give us character qualities such as brotherly kindness, humility, gentleness and patience. Knowing this, come to God with an open heart and give it to Him to lead.

A Godly Woman Loves God's Word

A godly woman must be spending time in God's Word and prayer. In this way, she will grow spiritually, and exchange worry or problems for His peace and the supply of her needs. Jeremiah 17:7-8 speaks about this strength from the Lord. There he describes a tree whose roots go deep down into the soil next to a river. When heat or drought come, the tree remains green and bears fruit.

Perhaps you have never studied the Bible in a serious way or don't know how to spend time with God in prayer. Begin by setting time aside each day to spend with Him, and do not let a busy schedule steal this time away from you. Many find that first thing in the morning, before the worries of the day crowd in, is a good time to meet with God. Devotional guides are available at Christian bookstores to help you understand the Bible and get used to reading it every day.[2]

If you are a new Christian, you might begin with the gospel of John. Otherwise, you might read through the New Testament, or the whole Bible, in a year. Read a chapter or two, and ask yourself three questions:

1. **What does this passage *say*?** What are the clear facts about the story or teaching?
2. **What does this passage *mean*?** Are there some verses I don't understand? Where can I find some answers?
3. **What does this passage *mean to me*?** In other words, how does this passage affect the way I live? What may I need to change? Is there a promise to remember? A command to obey? A sin to confess? What did I learn about God's character through this passage? Is there a special verse to memorise?

You may find it helpful to keep a small exercise book with your Bible to write down your thoughts, questions, and changes you want to make in your life. Later, you can look back and praise God for how He is helping you to grow.

As you spend time with God, you will also want to talk to Him about the daily needs and concerns you have for yourself and others. You will want to praise Him for His love and power, and thank Him for His work in your life. You will also want to listen to what He is saying to you through His Word. This is prayer—conversing with God. You can talk to God anytime or anywhere, but it is good to take quiet time each day just to share your heart with Him. Again, you can write out your concerns, needs, and praises in a small exercise book. Then remember to write down how God answers your prayers. In this way, your faith will grow.

A Godly Woman Loves Her Husband

You may be surprised to learn that married women are *commanded* to love their husbands. In Titus 2:4, the word Paul uses for love is not the sacrificial love of one Christian to another, but the mutual love of friends. If you are newly married, you may not ever imagine that the friendship you have with your husband could grow cold. You may not understand why wives must be reminded to love their husbands. But as a busy pastor's wife, mother, and perhaps working outside the home, you may find that time together with your husband is in short supply. A relationship that is not attended to can quickly wither. Paul reminds us to make our relationship with our husband a priority.

We all know that love binds two married people into one person, not just physically, but spiritually. If you feel that you do not have that kind of love for your husband, you must ask God for it. Lack of love will affect the whole family: yourself, your husband and the children. A heart that loves is always trying to protect and respond positively to her husband. She never speaks critically or negatively about him to anyone, including parents, closest friends and relatives. Love covers the faults and failures of others (Proverbs 10:12). If you have a problem with your husband, pray before you utter any word to him. God will enable you to be the kind of loving and supportive wife that He wants you to be.

A Godly Woman has a Submissive Spirit

As Christian wives, we are also called to submit to our husbands. God has appointed the man to be the loving head of the woman, and for her to submit to him (Ephesians 5:22, 25). For marriage to be smooth and to honour God, God said "... the head of every man is Christ, and the head of every woman is man, and the head of Christ is God" (1 Corinthians 11:3). The wife must choose to submit to her husband. She has to ask God to help her do this, knowing that her husband is responsible to Christ for his behaviour.

Even a pastor may be disobedient to the Word of God at times. The Apostle Peter makes it clear that a wife should submit even under those circumstances (1 Peter 3:1), unless he leads her to do things in direct contravention of God's Word. Submission may need to be done with prayer and tears, if the husband is not repentant. If your husband is violently abusive to you or your children, know that submission does not require you to continue to live in a situation where you feel you are in danger. Do not be ashamed to seek help from godly counsellors. You will not be the first pastor's wife who has had to do so.

A Godly Woman and Family Responsibilities

Titus 2:4 also commands mothers to love their children. Children are the responsibility of both parents, but the mother often carries more of the load and is closer to the children, especially when they are young. As mothers, we would all say that we love our children. But sometimes our lives say something else. We may become so busy with our jobs, church responsibilities and further training opportunities that our children never see us until just before bedtime. God wants us to make our children a priority in our lives.

Most importantly, the mother needs to teach the children the Word of God—not only to teach it but to live the life of a mother who loves God above all. Mothers who want to raise their children to love God above all must be able to live out God's truth in front of their children. Children learn much more from what we do than from what we say. So as Christian mothers, we should be very careful and pray about our daily walk, so that we may be good examples to our children and to everyone else.

Happy children are a blessing, but they are not the goal of our lives as mothers. We want to honour God in everything we do, and by example teach our children to do the same. Then our family will become a light for the gospel in our community.

A Godly Woman and Her Home

A home is not a nice building, nice furniture, nice food or anything you can see. A home is a home because it is made to be a home. A woman who loves God above all must know how to turn a house into a home. She can create a place where everyone is welcomed and made comfortable. As a wife and mother, we are the heart of the home—we set the tone that everyone feels as they enter. As our husband, children, and visitors come into our home, we can give a smile, a cheerful greeting, a warm hug, an encouragement, praise, and a listening ear. None of these cost anything except our time.

We also create a loving home by keeping it clean and orderly, decorating as our skills allow, and providing healthy meals for our family and guests. Our home can become a centre for ministry, as our heart for God becomes noticed by all who enter. God created women to appreciate beauty. Even a row of flowers along the veranda or some cheerful curtains in the window can communicate love and welcome to your family, as well as visitors.

A Godly Woman and Service

As godly women we are called to serve. Jesus gave us Himself as an example—He did not come to be served, but to serve (Matthew 20:28). As pastors' wives, we will see many opportunities in the church and community where we can serve, if we open our eyes. Dorcas was an example of a woman who was always doing good and helping the poor (Acts 9:36-43). We are also called by God to serve our husbands as partners (Genesis 2:18). We are not to compete with them or to lag behind them, but to work with them as a team as they lead the way.

A Godly Woman and Herself

It is possible for a pastor's wife to become so busy serving others that she forgets to look after herself. A woman who is tired, irritable and distracted by too many responsibilities is not very useful to her husband, her family, or God. In addition to feeding your spirit with regular time alone with God, remember to take care of yourself in other ways. Eat healthy meals, get enough sleep, and exercise regularly.

It is also possible to waste our days in front of the television, or communicating with friends on MXit or Facebook. We want to cultivate the character quality of diligence. Proverbs 14:23 says, "All hard work brings a profit, but mere talk leads only to poverty."

The Balancing Act

As you think about all of the priorities of the godly woman and pastor's wife, you may be thinking, "How can I do all of that at once?" You may feel that you are trying to balance many plates on a tray, and a few may fall and break! This is when your time with God becomes most important. As you spend time with Him, He will guide you with His Word and the Holy Spirit, to help you "order your steps" (Psalm 119:133).

Sometimes it helps to take a spiritual retreat with your husband, where you seek God's will for your plans for the year. He may show you new ministry opportunities. He may convict you that you are too busy and need to spend more time with your family. Ask Him to show you His purpose for your life and how to live that out in ordinary daily activities.

There are some practical things you can do to keep priorities in line and stay organized. Get a diary to write all of your appointments in, and then remember to use it! Plan your meals in advance, make a shopping list, and don't buy things on impulse while you are at the grocery store. You will save time and spend less money that way. Plan one special activity each week as a family, and write it in the schedule. Then your husband can truly say he already has an appointment at that time if other ministry opportunities arise.

When I was working, Friday was always set aside as family day. In the evening, my husband would not go into his study, and we would sit around playing games or sharing stories from the week—what happened with the children at school and with their friends. It was amazing what you could learn from the children by taking time with them. If I was working nights that week, I always let them know that I would not be available, but the next week we would be sure to have our family time again. The children all looked forward to our time together.

It is possible to balance a demanding career with family and ministry responsibilities, by depending on God for wisdom and strength. One well-known pastor's wife is the head of her own construction company, as well as a gifted Bible teacher and community leader. Yet she is described by those who know her as a submissive, loving wife and dedicated mother of three children. Her humility and servant's heart are evident as she cares for guests who visit her home.

In Colossians 3:23-24 is a good passage for employees, "Whatever you do, work at it with all your heart, as working for the Lord, not for men… It is the Lord Christ you are serving." Do not let church obligations or family be an excuse for poor performance or tardiness. Make a plan in advance how to handle certain situations that can arise unexpectedly. When I was working, I never missed a conference. I had to plan ahead and ask in time, but it always worked out. One nursing sister even changed her holiday time so I could go to my husband's graduation ceremony in the US. I believe this was possible because I was diligent when I was at work and I had good relationships with my colleagues and manager.

You will probably need help in the home if you are employed. Even if you are not employed outside the home, the ministry can be demanding. Housework may be difficult to handle alone. Learn how to manage your employees and plan their work for them. The Proverbs 31 woman didn't do it all herself. Children can also contribute to the housework, and it is a good character building opportunity for them. In our home, the house helper had a holiday during school breaks, and the children took over the housework.

The other thing that can help you balance home, ministry and work is to recognize and develop the gifts of other women in the church to work with you in ministry. Then you will be able to trust them to do the work, even when you are unable to be present. If employment or family responsibilities prevent you from being at every service, you do not need to feel guilty. If you are confident that you are doing what God has given you to do, then be happy with it. The important thing is that you and your husband are in agreement, and that he knows you support him completely from your heart.

I would like to share with you a testimony from Nonkululeko Eunice Rajuili, whose husband Moshe was involved in many different ministries over the years, from Area Director of Scripture Union, to seminary and Bible college principal, to pastor. She shares how she and her husband balanced their priorities when their children were young.

> Soon after we had settled *ilobolo* my husband paid me a longer visit to spend more time with his wife-to-be. In the middle of our casual conversation he brought in a business-like question. He wanted to know if I was prepared to be a stay-at-home-mum should God bless us with children. He went on to say he would like us to devote as much time to our children as possible in view of the fact children are a gift from God (Psalm 127:3).
>
> At that time I was an enthusiastic young teacher earning a monthly salary from the Department of Education. However, without any hesitation I readily said yes. I could read joy and satisfaction on his face. On my side, the positive response emanated from scriptural teachings I had received as well as my own upbringing. I grew up in a home where my mum would leave at six in the morning to go to work and be back at six in the evening. I experienced some secret loneliness in that situation. I so wished my mum could be home to have breakfast with us and welcome us in the afternoon. When we parted that day, my future husband and I had committed ourselves to be there not only for each other, but also for our children.
>
> As our three daughters were born, I readily took the role of being a stay-at-home mum in spite of the fact that my husband's salary as the travelling secretary of the Students Christian Movement (SCM) was minimal. This role brought many joys and sacrifices.
>
> First and foremost I had the joy of breastfeeding all our children. My husband came alongside me as a father by cooking oats or soft porridge to make sure I had enough milk. By staying

at home it meant I had plenty of time to do house chores, rest and breastfeed. It was indeed a wonderful experience. I did not have to worry about the sterilization of bottles or which was the best powder milk to buy.

Since I did not have to wake up to join the rat race, our morning atmosphere was relatively peaceful. As a wife and a mother I was there for both my husband and the baby. Having a mum at home gave the baby sufficient sleep. We would pray and have breakfast together. Occasionally, I would carry my baby on my back and go for short walks.

Spending twenty-four hours a day with the baby was both fulfilling and demanding. It came with baby talk, reading books and playing and laughing with the baby. Interestingly, one of the mothers in our church said she would be bored stiff if she were to stay at home. She wanted to know how I survived having to do "baby talk" the whole day. I didn't see it as a sacrifice—it was a joy, because it was where God wanted me to be at that moment. In the evening my husband would take over to give me time to prepare supper and rest. This teamwork enabled us to pray together, study the Bible together and have time for self-development. We had made a commitment that we were going to "strive to make each other great."

William Wordsworth, in one of his poems, says:

> *The world is too much with us: late and soon,*
> *Getting and spending, we lay waste our powers:*[3]

Wordsworth was referring to a world that is caught up in materialism. To choose to stay at home meant going against the current as far as materialism was concerned, and this drastic decision came with a lot of sacrifice.

One sacrifice I had to make was settling for a very simple wardrobe. Another was preparing very simple meals. I learned to be creative and organized, preparing dishes which were tasty and suited our pocket. We also lived in a house that was scantily furnished. At one stage we ended up with dining room chairs which were wobbly. A friend who visited us, when we warned her to be careful when she sat down, jokingly and innocently told us that she had been forewarned about our wobbly furniture.

My mother and my mother-in-law tried to talk me into going back to work several times. As an accounting teacher there was a demand for my skills. My friends would talk gleefully about the joys of earning a salary. In all these I chose to remain honest and resolute to the commitment I had made before we got married.

In conclusion, I would like to quote one of the songs we used to sing together as a duet, a song that was sung at our wedding:

> *It's not an easy road*
> *We are travelling to Heaven*
> *For many are the thorns on the way*
> *But Jesus walks beside me*
> *And brightens the journey*
> *And lightens every load* [4]

Indeed, it was a journey filled with joys and challenges. Our complete trust and dependence on God helped us to fulfil the commitment we had made to each other. The sacrifices were worth it. Today, our three daughters are grown, they love the Lord, and they are an asset to their communities. My husband was taken to be with the Lord in an accident recently, and the girls together decided that one of them would come back home to live with me as I adjusted. Our investment did bear fruit in the end—the joy that Moshe and I shared as parents continues to comfort me even today.

Not everyone would choose to make the sacrifices that this couple did. The most important thing is to be absolutely sure of God's leading. However you choose to balance all of your responsibilities as a pastor's wife, you will need to walk closely with God and ask him to help you. If you know what God's purpose for your life is, it will help you make choices to live the life that pleases him, whether you are employed outside the home or busy as a homemaker. The virtuous woman in Proverbs 31 had strength of character and strength of body so she could do many things. She was a woman who loved God above all and she walked with Him. You and I are called to be such women. We can do that only if we put God first and let Him lead us. He was faithful to those women of the Bible; He is still faithful to us today.

Questions to think about and discuss:

1. Study the following verses so that you will have confidence in your salvation and be able to share the gospel with others:

    a. Romans 3:23

    b. Romans 6:23

    c. 1 Peter 3:18

    d. Romans 10: 9,10

    e. Ephesians 2:8, 9

    f. John 10:27-29

    g. 1 John 5:11-12

2. Which of the nine priorities in this chapter do you think is the most important? How would you put them in order?

3. Are you living your life according to what you think is most important? Name one area you think you may need to change.

4. Write out how you spent your time each day this week. Based on your list, what would you say your priorities really are?

5. What can you do this week towards the priority of being devoted to God?

6. What qualities would you look for in a person you hire to look after your children or keep your home?

7. Spend some time this week thinking about God's priorities for your life. Plan to do at least one thing this week in each of these areas. Write it in your diary on the day you plan to do it. Then remember to look at your diary!

Discussion questions from this chapter are adapted from *Yes! I'm a Pastor's Wife, 2ⁿᵈ edition*, by Leah Marasigan Darwin (Makati, Philippines: Church Strengthening Ministry, Inc., 2007).

> When do I get time with the pastor? Do I need to make an appointment, too? I'm his wife!

> My husband is well-respected by all the women in the church. How can I compete?

> Where do the pastor and his wife go if *they* need counselling?

Chapter 5

Marriage and Ministry

Susan Binion

Being married to a man in ministry is a thrilling adventure of faith. It is not an ordinary life. A pastor's wife has the opportunity to partner with her husband as a midwife who brings spiritual children into the kingdom of God. She will witness the miracle of changed lives and the power of the gospel first-hand. Her faith will grow and stretch as challenges come her way.

But along with these blessings come difficulties. There are unique stresses on a ministry marriage, and a wise pastor's wife will work hard to see that her marriage is vibrant and growing, even in the midst of challenges. "The wise woman builds her house, but with her own hands the foolish one tears hers down" (Proverbs 14:1).

Basic Biblical Truths about Marriage

There is a verse in the Bible that gives the Biblical foundation on which every marriage rests. It is the only statement about marriage that is repeated four times in the Bible. Jesus used this passage in his answer to the Pharisees' question about divorce. It is a summary statement at the end of the passage on creation. It says, "For this reason a man will leave his father and mother and be united to his wife, and they will become one flesh" (Genesis 2:24). The writer of Genesis is giving a comment about the first marriage, that of Adam and Eve.

In his book, *I Married You*,[1] Walter Trobisch uses a triangle to describe a marriage on this firm foundation. He says that the three things essential to marriage are to *leave*, to *cleave* (be united) and to *become one flesh*. We can also think of a three-legged stool.

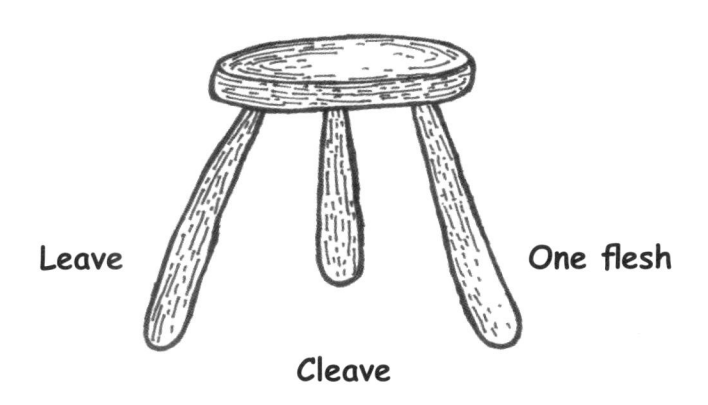

Leave **One flesh**

Cleave

To "leave father and mother" means leaving the authority of one's parents and making a fresh start as a family unit. "To cleave", or "to be united" means to stick to something like glue. The two people are now one, and cannot be separated without damage to both of them. They are closer to each other than they are to anyone else or anything else. This gives the marriage relationship priority over children, over relatives, even over the ministry. And finally, to "become one flesh" describes the physical aspect of marriage. The oneness that a married couple feels is expressed in physical union. When a couple expresses their love in physical intimacy, it unites them body, soul and spirit in a beautiful and mysterious way that God designed.

If any one of these three legs of the stool is missing or out of line, the stool—the marriage—is wobbly and likely to fall. Problems with in-laws or extended family, problems with one partner feeling neglected, problems with infidelity—in many cases these problems can be traced to a wobbly stool. Take some time to evaluate your marriage and see if your stool is stable.

Leah Marasigan-Darwin, in her book, *Yes! I'm a Pastor's Wife!*[2], talks about two keys to a successful marriage—**Respect** and **Romance**. These keys unlock the secret to our husbands' hearts. They will help us to keep our marriage stool from wobbling.

Respect

When I was about to marry, an older woman sat me down to give me some advice. Her marriage had almost come apart some years before, and she wanted to share with me the truth from Scripture that saved her marriage. She opened her Bible to Ephesians 5:33: "Each one of you (husbands) also must love his wife as he loves himself, and the wife must respect her husband." In the Amplified Bible, respect goes by many names: reverence, notice, regard, honour, prefer, venerate, esteem, defer to, praise, love and admire exceedingly. I copied each of these words onto a bookmark which I still keep in my Bible. It reminds me how important this command is to God, to my husband, and to the success of our marriage.

As a pastors' wife, you may have noticed that there are many people who admire and respect your husband. You may have also noticed that many of them are young and beautiful! There could be a danger here, if our husbands feel more respect from others than they do from us. As Linda Dillow, author of *Creative Counterpart*, says, to be a wise woman who builds her marriage, you must be the president of your husband's "fan club".[3]

One way to show respect and admiration for our husbands is to build them up with encouraging words. Proverbs 18:21 says, "The tongue has the power of life and death." We need to be using words that give life to our husbands. We can tear them down so easily by always trying to correct their flaws and show them how they are wrong in some area. We are not our husbands' Holy Spirit! Rather let us ask the Holy Spirit to help us to see the strengths and gifts God has given our husbands, and to build them up with our words.

Of course, every marriage thrives on open communication. If there is an area that you see in your husband's life that is harming your relationship or his ministry, pray about the best way to approach your husband. Share with him in an honest, loving way. But remember that words of affirmation are even more important.

One marriage counselor said, "Affirmation is everything. When a man is affirmed, he can conquer the world." If a man knows his wife believes in him, he will have confidence to try new things and improve in every area of his life.[4]

Each culture has different ways of showing respect. Each person has ways that he or she prefers to be treated. Study your husband and figure out what will communicate your respect to him in the best way. Then don't delay—do it!

We may not realize how vital respect is to our husbands' self-worth. After interviewing hundreds of men for her book, *For Women Only*, Shaunti Feldhahn found that a man sees love and respect as almost the same thing. Respect and admiration say, "I love you" to a man.[5] If you don't believe this, try giving your husband an "I Respect You" card and list all the things you admire and respect about him. You may be surprised at the response you receive.

Romance

The other key to unlocking our husbands' heart and strengthening our marriages is to make passion a priority in our relationship. Dr. James Dobson points out that married women have three roles in the home—that of a loving *wife*, who diligently maintains the home, a caring *mother*, who looks after the children's needs, and seductive *mistress* who enjoys giving her husband pleasure through physical intimacy.[6] Often these three roles are at odds with each other. After keeping up with children all day, cooking, cleaning, and possibly working outside the home, we do not feel very passionate towards our husbands.

The same woman who told me about the secret of respecting my husband told me something else. "Say yes as often as you can to your husband's sexual advances. Nothing cuts his heart more deeply than to be refused or to feel that you are not excited to be physically intimate with him." A fulfilling sex life gives a man the strength and well-being to face the world with confidence. It is not just a physical need, but an emotional one.

As a Christian woman, you may not be used to talking about these issues. Churches have not always been open about discussing sexual intimacy in marriage. But God doesn't have a problem with it. The Song of Solomon very clearly describes the joy of married love. Genesis 2:25 points out that Adam and Eve were naked, but they felt no shame. The goal of our marriage relationship should be complete trust and openness with each another in every aspect of our lives, including physical intimacy.

If you have ever been sexually abused or raped, you may find sexual intimacy with your husband is very painful emotionally. There is hope for your situation through counselling and the healing power of the Holy Spirit. God promises a crown of beauty instead of ashes, and a garment of praise instead of a spirit of despair (Isaiah 61:3). He can redeem this painful situation for His glory, and give you a satisfying sex life with your husband.

Men and women respond differently to physical expressions of love. You will need to communicate in order to meet one another's needs. There are many Christian books with helpful information and practical ideas to light the fires of passion in your marriage. If your relationship is struggling in this area, don't be afraid to get help.

So, what are some practical ideas to help turn the dutiful housewife into a passionate lover once the children are in bed for the night? The main thing to remember is that romance takes planning. Make sure you have time each day to communicate about the day's events. Weekly times away from the family and ministry responsibilities build your relationship and help you to feel more responsive toward your husband. Go for a walk in the neighbourhood or a local mall. Go to a nearby park and relax with a picnic.

A surprise weekend away, a romantic dinner after the children have gone to sleep, even backrubs—all of these communicate our love for our husbands and don't have to be expensive. Write love notes and put them in the pocket of his jacket or leave them in his desk drawer. Send loving messages with your cell phone. Ask God to help you be creative with the resources that you have.

Keeping physically fit—eating well and exercising—improve your general health and attitude to life in all areas. Men are attracted by what they see. Do you work at looking your best for your husband?

Your husband can get a secretary. You can hire a housekeeper. But only you can fulfill your husband's need for sexual intimacy. So go and enjoy sex with your husband in the fulfilling way that God designed—you can start tonight!

Catch the Foxes

Song of Songs 2:15 says,

> Catch for us the foxes,
> the little foxes
> that ruin the vineyards,
> our vineyards that are in bloom.

There are many little foxes that can threaten your marriage relationship. By regularly setting aside time to tend the vineyard of your relationship, you will notice the foxes and be able to chase them away before they cause too much destruction. "But," you say, "I can't get my husband to slow down enough to talk about these things." Remember how Esther prepared two delicious meals before she presented her plea to her husband? I am confident that God will give you the creative ability to approach your husband with these important matters.

As a pastor's wife, you may find **financial pressures** eating away at your peace and stability at home. As a couple, you must agree on the ways you spend money and talk freely about your finances. We have given a whole chapter to this issue (see Chapter 8), as financial disagreements are one of the leading causes of strife in marriage.

In-laws and extended family relationships can cause problems in a marriage, especially if the couple cannot agree on how to handle the situation. This is where the "leave" leg of the stool may make the marriage wobble. Agrippa Khathide, in his book, *Bone of my Bones*,[7] describes leaving as an emotional and physical break from the parents. He says the couple must have some measure of autonomy to decide the destiny of the new family and live out the covenant they have made to each other. Every situation from long-term visitors in the home to deciding where the children will spend their summer holiday is made smoother if the couple holds their covenant with each other in the highest esteem. Our extended family is a great blessing from God, and we need to honour our parents. But a couple must establish their identity as a separate family as well.

Another problem ministry marriages often face is that of **busyness**. One ministry wife talks about her busy pastor husband:

> Immediately after [accepting the call to ministry], my husband literally consumed himself with church ministry; everything else in his life came secondary, including our family. Access to his schedule was scarce; he was either in prayer, preaching, at a wedding or funerals. Of course, this was hard adjusting to, because there were house errands that needed his attention but he would be swarmed with ministerial duties or his work. You can imagine a case where I am livid at my husband yet I have to listen and encourage him while he is preaching.

Some pastors' wives are busier than their husbands. If you are trying to balance family, ministry, further academic studies and employment, time to nurture your marriage will be scarce. A friend of mine once explained that an orchid must be watered in a special way. If you let it get dry and then drown it with water once a week, it will wither and die. An orchid doesn't need much water, but it needs it every day. Our marriages are the same way. A little bit of tenderness and attention every day can go a long way toward preventing problems in a marriage.

Some have said that the **threat of infidelity** is greater in a ministry marriage. Why might that be? We have already discussed the admiring crowd that may have your husband on a pedestal. There is also the issue of counselling female church members privately. If the husband is an evangelist, he may travel frequently away from home. Another possibility is the wife's own temptation to infidelity. A husband who seems to put the ministry and everyone else's needs above the needs of his wife and family could leave her feeling lonely and open to the attention shown by more "sensitive" men.

Sadly, it does sometimes happen that a pastor is unfaithful to his wife. Being a submissive wife does not mean that you ignore the problem and hope that it goes away. In these days of HIV/AIDS and other sexually transmitted diseases, it is an urgent matter, because you could be exposing yourself to infection. You must speak openly and honestly with your husband and approach the appropriate church leadership. You will need to use protection if you have intercourse with your husband until the behaviour stops and he has tested negative for HIV.

Discuss the above dangers with your husband and agree on guidelines to prevent infidelity in your marriage. The moral failure of a pastor (or his wife) can destroy more than a marriage and family. It can destroy a church and bring shame to the name of Jesus. Although there is always forgiveness and redemption to be found in confession of sin, some consequences can never be reversed.

Because of the financial pressures that often go along with being a pastor, it happens that sometimes **pastors and their wives don't live together**. Perhaps the pastor is assigned to a rural church far from town, and the wife's employment is in the city. Sometimes the pastor is assigned to a city far from where the couple had been living, and the wife can't get a job transfer. These are difficult economic times, and a person with a job could be considered a fool for giving it up.

The problem is, if we do not physically live with our husband, it is difficult to cleave to him. It is difficult to develop our marriage relationship into the beautiful picture of Christ's relationship with the church described in Ephesians 5 if we rarely spend time together. Can a couple keep the marriage stool from wobbling with text messages and phone conversations alone?

There are many reasons that a husband and wife may need to live apart for a limited time. But sometimes I think a wife may fail to cleave to her husband because of her own fears about God's ability to provide for her family's needs. Ultimately, whose responsibility is it to provide for our family? Is it possible that we could do with less, and make our marriage more of a priority?

Some Bible college students travelled to Mozambique to visit alumni and other pastors who were working cross-culturally under difficult conditions. In each case, the wife was working wholeheartedly alongside her husband in the ministry. The students marveled at the wives' dedication and the effective ministry the couples had together. The single male students remarked that they had always hoped to marry a professional woman with a good job who could support them financially in their ministry. Now they hoped they could find a wife willing to follow them wherever the Lord led, even if it meant living in a remote place under difficult circumstances.

Grace Kimati shares a story in her book, *Courting in Marriage*,[8] about a woman who felt that she had to work to supplement her husband's income. But by the time she calculated the cost of transport to work, hiring a housekeeper and child minder, as well as her "executive wardrobe", she discovered that the little bit of income she had left over was not worth the cost to her marriage and family relationships. Living apart is dangerous to a marriage. If you must live apart for a time, be sure that you are both willing to work hard to overcome those dangers.

When it is Not Ideal

It happens in every marriage, even ministry marriages, that serious problems come along that seem to have no solution. As a pastor's wife, you may feel that your marriage is supposed to be perfect, and you could never admit to anyone that you need help. But Christian growth happens as we interact with others who have been down the road we are walking. As a couple, try to find an older couple in ministry that you both trust to mentor you along the way. Develop a friendship so that when difficult times come you have somewhere to turn. If your marriage is struggling, get help. It is not a sign of weakness, but of great strength and courage, to do so. It shows that you are willing to do whatever it takes to keep the promises you made to God and to your husband on your wedding day.

Walter Trobisch says, "The testimony which you give with your own married life does more than a hundred lectures on marriage."[9] Ask God to help you and your husband develop a marriage that will demonstrate God's grace and love in action to a hurting world.

Questions to think about and discuss:

1. Which leg of the marriage stool, "leave", "cleave", or "one flesh" is most wobbly in your marriage? Which is most stable?
2. What are ways in your culture that you can show respect to your husband?
3. How could you show your husband that you are the president of his "fan club"?
4. Did you have any "honeymoon counselling" before you got married? What kind of expectations and attitudes did you bring to the marriage bed?
5. Which of the ways mentioned to light up the passion in your marriage do you think are possible for you? Which one will you plan to do soon?
6. What particular "foxes" do you and your husband need to catch to keep your marriage safe?
7. If husband and wife must live apart for a time, what are some ways that they could keep their relationship alive and model a committed Christian marriage to their children and community?

Discussion questions from this chapter are adapted from *Yes! I'm a Pastor's Wife, 2nd edition*, by Leah Marasigan Darwin (Makati, Philippines: Church Strengthening Ministry, Inc., 2007).

> Our children have grown up "playing church". When will their faith become real to them?

> Everyone at church expects the pastor's children to be perfect. Their children aren't perfect!

> Why should I listen to what my father says about God? He never has time to listen to *me*.

Chapter 6

Children, Family Life and Ministry

Christine Phumelele Xaba

Perhaps you have heard the saying, "The hand that rocks the cradle rules the world." There is no doubt that when it comes to the home and children, a mother has tremendous influence in the lives of her children and the moulding of their characters, especially when they are young. As I think back over my own life and all of the people who influenced me, I am amazed to realise that most of them were mothers. My own mother loved me very much, but she was not educated or a believer. So I am thankful that God put many Christian women in my life as well.

When my husband and I got married I lost my job because I had to change my place of residence. I could not work in the new country unless I underwent some training again. So I became a full time housewife after getting married. I was not pleased about that, as there was a great need for me to work. My husband was a pastor and was not receiving enough financial support to meet the needs of the family. But our living God had His plan in our situation. I was at home until all our children were born and were up to school-going age. This was the best time I had with the children and the family. I also had time to train at Bible school for four years—something I had long wanted to do. God used this time to prepare me for His service.

Walk and Talk

A Christian mother must be a good example to her children by both word and action. First, she must have a deep love for God's Word. This deep love must be demonstrated most of all in her own home, with her own children. Elizabeth George, in her book, *A Woman After God's Own Heart*, says that we have an "assignment from God" to teach His Word to our children.[1] This assignment is found in Deuteronomy 6:6-8 and Proverbs 1:8, where we see both father and mother involved in teaching their children God's Word. God uses His Word to draw our children to Himself. In Romans 10:17, the apostle Paul emphasizes that "faith comes from hearing the message, and the message is heard through the word of Christ." So by teaching the Word of God to our children we give them a good and profitable start in life. God promises us that His Word shall not return to Him void (Isaiah 55:11). What we plant in their little hearts, God will cause to grow. Even when they grow up into adulthood and have to leave their parents' homes, they will remember what they have learned.

A mother must also teach her children about God's wisdom. Wisdom is knowledge at work in practical ways in our life. It is being able to apply God's Word in different situations to live right and make good decisions. In Proverbs 31:1-9 we read about a mother who shared God's wisdom with her son. This young man listened well and remembered her godly advice as he grew to manhood.

We must also be praying mothers. Stormie Omartian, in her book, *The Power of a Praying Parent*,[2] gives many good ideas about the kinds of things you can pray for your children. God chose us for this ministry and He is faithful to walk with us in everything. You can also teach your children to pray and love God's word. Choose a time and place where you sit with the children, read a Bible story with them, teach them a memory verse and pray with them every day. Give them prayer requests that you want them to pray for. When God has answered a request, tell them and thank God together with them. Scripture Union provides devotional guides for all ages of children. Your local Christian bookseller will have many other books to help you as well. Make use of these resources as you teach your children.[3]

Our children are learning from us every moment of every day. In Deuteronomy 6:4-9, God tells parents to take every opportunity to teach their children about His commands, using everyday events as life lessons. I once heard of a girl who said to her mother: "You cannot tell me to do that when you do not do it yourself. There is nothing you can tell me." So mothers, we must "walk our talk" and be a good example of what a Christian mother should be.

It is true that some pastors' wives are working secular jobs, but they must try to have time for their families, children and ministry. Our God knows about our situations and is able to give us strength and wisdom to fulfil all the roles that He has assigned to us as pastors' wives. When the children are grown up and have seen things with their own eyes, their view of God can change. I once heard of a pastor's family where the children did not want to hear anything about Christ and the church. It seems the pastor never spent time with the family. He was only concerned with the church members and their children, not about his own family. You will never regret making time for your family, even with the busy schedule you have.

Mothers in the Bible

The Bible tells us about a number of women who taught their children about God, His Word and His wisdom. In Exodus 2:2-10 we are told about Moses' mother who took care of her baby and hid him to save him from being killed. She taught her daughter how to watch him when he was placed in a basket at the river bank, as well as how she should offer to get a nurse for him should he be found by anyone that wanted to keep him. Eventually, Moses was found by Pharaoh's daughter and given back to his mother to take care of him until he was of age. She taught him about the God of the Hebrews and His promises to His people. Moses never forgot those lessons he learned at home. He was saved for God's purpose—to free the Israelites from slavery.

In 1 Samuel 1:20-28 we are told about Hannah, Samuel's mother. She prayed, making a promise to God to give her son back to God from his childhood to serve in the tabernacle. She was faithful to keep her promise. Samuel became a great prophet of God.

We are not told about Daniel's mother, but from the life he lived we can see that he was taught about the living God of Israel and His miracles. He never departed from those teachings, even though separated from his family in a foreign land.

The "Preacher's Kid"

Pastors' children are not perfect, but sometimes the church members can expect them to be. When they are very small, the pastor's child may rush up to the father while he is preaching. Perhaps as they get older, they may get into some trouble at school and all the community hears about it. How do we handle this?

We must understand that children of ministry families live their lives in front of the whole community. Yet, they are still children, and children learn by making mistakes. Most of all, we must show them unconditional love, no matter what they have done wrong. "God demonstrates his own love for us in this: While we were still sinners, Christ died for us" (Romans 5:8). We must love our children the same way God loves us. We must not withhold our love and acceptance until they behave, but love them even with their mistakes. There must always be a way back home for them, just like the prodigal son.

On the other hand, we need to take our job of parenting seriously, and take time to learn how to bring up our children God's way, with discipline *and* love. If we are training them well at home, they will usually respond well in public situations. We do not have to shout and punish the children all the time, but the child must know his or her mother's actions and facial expressions and respond to them because the church and the community take the pastors' children as examples, whether good or bad. There are many good Christian books written about raising children in a way that pleases the Lord. Take time to read them together with your husband, and agree how you will handle difficult situations.[4]

Children in ministry families also need to develop as individuals, and not be required to fit into some mould of who a pastor's child should be. It is who they are at their very core—who God created them uniquely to be—that matters, not their identity as the pastor's child. Ask God to help you see your children with *His* eyes, as He "knit them together" in your womb. What are the plans *He* has for your child's life? What has God written in *His* book for your child? How can you help your child discover it? (Psalm 139:13-16)

One pastor's wife explained that her teenage daughter complained about their strict family rules at home, and blamed it on being the pastor's daughter. Her mother responded that their family rules were based on the Bible and would be the same whether she was the pastor's daughter or not. Be sure that you can justify your expectations of your children based on Scripture and what will please Jesus. Never tell your children they must behave a certain way because of what other people will say.

On the other hand, our children must understand that there are many different cultures, each with its own standards. If an urban family has been assigned to a rural church, they may find that the way they dress and interact with others will have to change. Showing respect to adults is always appropriate. Teach your children how to behave when visitors come. Greeting them respectfully, turning off the television, offering to get a drink—all of these actions will make the gospel attractive to others. Help your children see the need to become partners with you in becoming "all things to all people," so that together you may win some to Jesus (I Corinthians 9:22-23).

The greatest need a pastor's child has is to know Jesus as his personal Saviour and to live his life to please Him above all. Growing up at church every time the doors are open can sometimes hinder a child's understanding of the gospel, or cause him to think he is "OK" with God because he knows all the right answers. Having a personal faith in Jesus will help our children to cope with some of the difficult and painful things that come along the way. They will be able to separate church issues and hurtful people from their relationship with God, and so will not reject Him later in life.[5]

When Problems Come

Catherine and her pastor husband had done all they could do concerning child upbringing. But some of their children's behaviour was so appalling it resulted in criticism from the congregation. They blamed Catherine for the behaviour of those children. This hurt the parents deeply. In their hearts they knew they had done their best. When such a situation arises it is so easy for a pastor's wife to feel she is to blame for what their children turn out to be. But we need to realise that children are human beings who have freedom to choose what they want to be. As they grow into adults, those choices may be painful to us, but we can only turn our children over to their heavenly Father to deal with them as He sees best.

Sometimes children in a ministry family feel that they grow up under very poor conditions because the church does not care about their father and the ministry. Especially if the father was working a secular job before joining the ministry, the children may feel deprived of certain things. Our children will adopt our attitudes towards people in the church and our material possessions. Do they see us trusting God, and looking to Him, not church members, for our provision? Are we displaying hope and contentment with our situation?

As parents in the home we must also remember we do not discuss any misunderstanding in front of the children, whether the misunderstanding is between us, about the church, about church members or anyone else. We must respect our children and avoid telling them in great detail things that do not go right at the church or things that hurt us. They will be hurt and grow bitter towards the people concerned.

If and when we come across big problems, we may tell our children if they are grown up and understand the Word of God and the ministry well. As we pray with them about these problems, they will see God work and their faith will grow. But we must do all this in love (Romans 12:1-2; 9-21). Paul emphasizes the importance of doing things in love. We do not have this kind of love by nature but we get it from God through prayer and searching His Word. If we submerge ourselves in the pool of His love and we acknowledge that His ways are wise and that they work when we are faithful to follow His instruction, then our ministry can have an impact beyond measure.

As parents we have daily opportunities in our homes to plant God's Word deeply in the minds and souls of our children. We must always remember that we have the blessed privilege of tending their hearts and bringing them up in the training and instruction of the Lord—Ephesians 6:4. The little hearts that God has placed in our care are treasures indeed.

By having a passion for teaching God's Word and His wisdom, and by being faithful to Him in word and deeds, we can minister to our children. If they see that we love God and are committed to the work that He has called us to do, they will feel the same about it. If we do our work lovingly and faithfully our children will walk with us—and they will have the privilege of being partners in God's work in the lives of others.

Questions to think about and discuss:

1. What are some of the blessings of being a pastor's child?

2. What are some of the difficulties of being a pastor's child?

3. What one thing will you choose to do today to help your children learn to love God's Word and desire a personal relationship with Him?

4. What can you do to improve your parenting skills?

5. What can you do to prevent your children from becoming bitter towards God or the church?

6. How can you help your children see God's plan for their life and give them a vision for serving Him?

> What if there is nothing in the cupboard when someone knocks?

> I live at the Mission Station. People are always at the door. What can I do?

> I think my children are beginning to resent all these visitors.

Chapter 7

Hospitality: Opening Our Hearts and Homes

Christine Phumelele Xaba

As a pastor's wife, you can be sure that you will have many opportunities to welcome people into your home. It sounds easy—just open one's house to people, prepare good meals for them to eat and a comfortable bed for them to sleep in. But hospitality is not only that. It is a ministry by itself—it is the work of love. It comes from a heart that is full of God's love towards any person who is in need. Whether the need is spiritual, social, physical, or emotional, the person at your door needs attention and care.

As Christian women and pastors' wives we must ask God to give us His love and to develop our minds so we can do His will in the area of hospitality. We need to be women who love God above all, choosing to love Him with all our hearts and all our might. We need to ask God every day and all the time to work in us through the Holy Spirit to lead and guide us and to do everything with us.

Give Ourselves to God

In Romans 12:1-2, the Apostle Paul urges Christians to give themselves to God.

> Therefore, I urge you brothers, in view of God's mercy, to offer your bodies as living sacrifices, holy and pleasing to God—this is your spiritual act of worship. Do not conform any longer to the pattern of this world, but be transformed by the renewing of your mind.

"Urge" is a very strong word. It means, "I hope you will take to heart and make your own the things I am about to say." Paul asks them to "offer their bodies as living sacrifices." This means that there is no part of their body that is going to be left out. I must give my entire self—hands, feet, even my eyes. If God shows me a need, I must be willing to do something about it. Every part of my body is to be used by Him according to His will. I am a "living sacrifice" for Him to use as He sees best.

In verse 2 Paul says that we must be transformed by the renewing of our minds. This work is only done by God through the Holy Spirit who lives in us as Christians. We must ask God to transform our heart attitude so that we can love people with His love and see with spiritual eyes. Hospitality is not just opening our homes to care for the physical needs of people. It is doing things that will touch lives and bring people to Christ.

Give Ourselves to Others

The first commandment is to love God with all our heart, soul, mind and strength. The second is to love our neighbour as ourselves (Matthew 22:37-39). Once we have opened our hearts to God to use us, it becomes easy for us to open our homes to people.

Paul encourages us to share with God's people in need and practice hospitality (Romans 12:13). As a leader in the church, we are expected to be hospitable (1 Timothy 3:2). While some are equipped with a special gift of hospitality, all of us are expected to welcome people into our home. We do not have to have special training to do this, but just listen to the Holy Spirit speaking to us quietly in our hearts.

Love Above All

Karen Mains has written a book about hospitality called, *Open Heart, Open Home*.[1] I have learned that it is possible to open the door of your house without opening the door of your heart. If you are irritated at being interrupted when someone knocks on your door, it will show on your face. On the other hand, people can be touched with the spirit of love and hospitality that is in your house, even if you have little physically to offer. Do everything with love. What use is it to give someone food and a bed, and not to give them love? We do not have the right to choose people because of who they are and what they look like. We have to take care of everyone according to their need.

When we got married, my husband was a pastor of a rural church in an inland area. The people did not know anything about cleanliness. They walked long distances from their homes to the Mission Station where we lived. If they needed accommodation they would go to bed dirty as they were. I was still young and scared to tell them to wash before going to bed. This worried me and I prayed about it. The way God answered my prayer was not by stopping them from coming to our house, or by making them wash before going to bed. Instead He did it by changing my heart. He gave me a heart full of love and compassion. I loved them and accepted them as they were.

This is not the only time that God brought people to our home because he had a lesson to teach us. We began inviting needy children to stay in our home. In fact, we always seemed to have more children than beds! Our children learned to share. Now our son is grown, and his house is always full of people who need help. We thank God for that.

Sometimes you do not have to give anything to the person who has a problem. Your visit, presence and touch can bring healing and comfort far greater than words. You can always give a smile, a warm greeting and a touch, a hug, and a friendly call by name where that is acceptable. The way you treat others is a sermon in itself, and shows them that you are a child of God.

God wants us to be ready to be used by Him all the time and everywhere we are. Being willing to take time in the middle of our busy day to help someone could save a life. A friend of mine phoned me some years ago and told me that she was hurting emotionally so much that she had decided to take her life. She mentioned that she meant to take her car keys and go to commit suicide. But instead of taking the car keys she took the telephone and phoned me. I was shocked, but God helped me to speak to her. We prayed over the phone and we cried together. Our good Lord heard our prayers and rescued her. She is still living today and loves the Lord very much.

You may find that some problems come from people in the church. The church members may have expectations on the way they should be treated when they come for a visit. Still give them love. Offer what you have. Do not allow yourself to become bitter towards them. Be bold to make things right with everyone. Do not go a long way with something in your heart that spoils your ministry or that hinders you from being comfortable when meeting someone. Be welcoming to everyone, wherever you find them. The Word of God urges us to live at peace with everyone (Romans 12:18).

Be Observant

A person with a hospitable heart will notice the needs around her. Many years ago, before I got married, a young Christian lady phoned me early in the morning. She told me that she had seen me at a meeting the previous night, and I did not look happy at all. I was surprised that she saw me because we were watching a movie in that service and the room was dark. She wanted to see me that same day. I didn't know her well, but God wanted to use her to meet my needs.

When we met, I told her my needs and my problems. She promised to tell her mother about my needs. She also told me that her mother was in a prayer group in her church and they would pray for me. Her mother shared my needs with her prayer group. As they prayed the Lord laid it on their hearts to help me. They did big and wonderful things for me, meeting every one of my needs. The Holy Spirit had taught her to be on the lookout for anyone who had a need. We must ask God to help us to be observant wherever we go.

Looking Beyond Our Front Door

Many people in our communities go hungry and even die around us, but we do not feel any special compassion towards them. Sometimes we do not even know or see them. Perhaps they are sick with HIV or AIDS, and we think they may be receiving judgment from God. This is when we need God's eyes, ears and heart to see, hear and feel their pain with them. Only then will we be able to "love our neighbor as ourselves."

A few years ago one teacher from a high school phoned me and told me about three children who were orphaned and did not have anyone staying with them. She told me that at times they went to school without having eaten. Sometimes they did not go to school because they did not have soap to wash their school uniform. I did not know this teacher, the school or the children. I visited the school, and while speaking to the principal she told me about other children who were in the same situation. I prayed about this because I really did not know what to do. I had no money to help them. But God intervened. I got help from the Social Welfare Society and from another man who took the matter to his church, and they supported these children.

The social worker asked me how I had come to know about these children because they do not live or go to school in my area. She asked if I was a Christian. By this act of caring, the message of God's love went out to quite a number of people. So we as Christian women and pastors' wives must have ears to hear about people's needs and hearts full of God's love to fulfill His call for us.

The Blessings of Showing Hospitality

We must ask God to help us to be generous givers. This is not an easy thing to do, and at times we feel that we do not have anything to give to people. But sometimes God brings a person to our door because He wants to meet *our* need.

One lady went to visit a certain pastor and his wife during Christmas. They went to town because this visitor wanted to see the town, and she bought some things to take back home. When she bought things for herself, she also bought the same for the pastor's wife. When they returned home, the pastor's family was very surprised to receive so many things from this visitor: clothing, shoes, jewellery and ornaments. God wanted to bless them with Christmas presents through this lady. The Bible says that when we welcome strangers, we are sometimes entertaining angels without knowing it (Hebrews 13:2). This lady was not an angel, but she was surely sent by God to encourage this pastor's wife.

We find a similar example in Joshua 2:3-21. There, a woman by the name of Rahab opened her door to the Israelite spies. She was known as a bad woman, but God wanted to use her to save the lives of these men. Through her they were protected from being killed, and her family was protected when the city of Jericho was destroyed. God saved Rahab and her family when she opened her door to strangers.

In Genesis 17:1-9 we are told of Abraham who welcomed the angels from heaven not knowing that it was God bringing him good news—the promise that his wife, Sarah, was going to give birth to a son in a year's time. This reminds me of a man in Gauteng who wanted to come to see my husband. We did not know this man, and we did not have anything to give to him. We did not know it at the time, but we later realized that God was bringing him to meet our need. We welcomed him with pleasure. While he and my husband were talking my husband's phone rang. He could not hear the caller, but kept saying "Hello? Hello?" The visitor said, "Your phone is too old, Mfundisi!" He took my husband to a shop where he bought my husband a new phone. We were greatly surprised in the way God met our need.

Prepare for Guests

There is a proverb which says that people who live in the city sleep with an empty pot. In other words, they do not live as if they expect (or would even like to have) visitors. But where I grew up, a visitor was always welcomed and given something to eat, whether we were expecting him or not. So now, I always offer our visitors something to drink, along with sandwiches or cakes, if we have them. Because we often have visitors, I always cook a little extra at supper time, just in case. And if the visitors are many, our children know that they are the ones who will take a smaller portion.

If the visitors are just from across town, it may not be necessary to cook for them. But if they have travelled far, I always try to prepare something for them to eat. I keep some rice and chutney and a tin of fish on hand at all times—it is something that is quick and easy to prepare for unexpected guests.

As pastor's wives, God has called and assigned us for a special purpose. He wants us to live lives that touch other people. Opening our hearts and homes to other people is a way to do this. Let us not lose hope, but let us run the race and do the work that God has called us to do. God has promised to neither leave us nor forsake us, but to rather walk with us as long as we are faithful to Him. Let us open our hearts and our homes for any one in need, until we receive the reward that He has prepared for us at the end of our journey.

Questions to think about and discuss:

1 Describe a time when you had to rely on someone's hospitality unexpectedly.

2 What are some of the cultural expectations about welcoming visitors where you are from?

3. What are some of the difficulties about welcoming visitors? What are some of the blessings?

4. What does the Bible say about welcoming visitors?

5. What are some of the ways we can prevent our children from resenting unexpected guests?

6. How does our heart attitude affect our family's view of visitors?

7. What are some practical ways that we can prepare for unexpected guests on a limited budget?

> How can I trust God more in the area of our finances?

> Things seemed easier when my husband had a secular job.

Chapter 8

Managing the Family Finances

Fikile Octavia Mpunzana

The Bible paints a beautiful picture of a person who trusts in the Lord. That person will be like a tree planted by a flowing stream, whose leaves are always green and whose branches never fail to bear fruit. The Bible calls this person *blessed* (Jeremiah 17:7-8). It is a blessing to be a pastor's wife whose success comes from a Christ-centred life. She doesn't have to spend her entire life chasing riches. She seeks only the presence of God.

In 2 Kings 4 we read the story of the prophet's widow who was in serious financial difficulty. Elisha asked her, "What do you have in your house?" With a little oil and a collection of empty jars, she demonstrated her faith in God, and He provided abundantly for her needs. As a pastor's wife you have resources that God can use to bless you economically. He will empower those that He can trust. You can become a woman of action whose secret weapon is your relationship with God.

As a woman of action, do not stretch out your hands for hand-outs from other people. Allow God to touch their hearts by bringing their tithes and offerings into the house of the Lord. Discourage a dependency syndrome. Be an example of trusting God and demonstrate that He is our source of income.

Mfundisi Ndobe was a teacher and lived a comfortable life. Then he and his wife were called into God's ministry. Things became difficult financially. The pastor decided to go back to his career, but his wife encouraged him to trust in the Lord for every aspect of their lives. God moved a certain doctor in the church to pay all the fees, uniforms and transport to school for their children. The entire church learned from him to support the pastor and his family. That happened through prayer, fasting and trusting in God. God who has called you is faithful. He provides for everything you need in the ministry (1 Corinthians 1:9).

Seek First the Kingdom of God

Financial growth is often linked to spiritual growth in God's kingdom. God knows that it is dangerous to put great wealth into the hands of someone who is too spiritually immature to handle it. When people get money and use it to sin, it does them more harm than good (Proverbs 1:32).

The foundation of financial security is a lifestyle built on the Word of God. Godly prosperity is the result of putting God's Word—all of it, not just the part about money—first place in your life. In Matthew 6:25-33, Jesus said, "Seek first his kingdom and his righteousness, and all these things will be given to you as well." To seek God's kingdom requires repentance and believing the good news. No one can see the kingdom of God without being born again (John 3:3). If you have never taken this first step in your relationship with God, you can do so today (See Chapter 4).

As a born again pastor's wife, your responsibility is not to seek after prosperity but to seek His kingdom and His righteousness and to obey His Word. God knows your physical needs as well as your spiritual needs, and he will provide. To have true prosperity, love must be the guiding force of your life. Every right action you take, every godly decision you make—praying for your enemies instead of hating them, blessing instead of cursing—makes you more like Christ and opens the doors to spiritual and physical blessing from God (1 Peter 3:8-11).

Peter reminds us in his first letter that sometimes it is possible for Christians to suffer for their faith. In some countries, a person who confesses Christ may lose his job or a chance at a good education. There are times when there does not seem to be any earthly reward for doing good. But God promises that we will be overjoyed in his presence when his glory is revealed, and we will experience the blessing of comfort from the Holy Spirit even now (1 Peter 4:12-16).

A Pastor's Wife Is a Steward

God owns everything. Everything you have, even things you may think you have earned, belong to Him. You may work and get a salary, but the money is God's money. You are a steward of what God has given you, and you want to be found faithful (1 Corinthians 4:2). A steward is one who manages another person's property. As a pastor's wife God has entrusted you with natural abilities, spiritual resources and material possessions. His Word guides you in how to use them.

A key element of stewardship is giving of oneself first. Paul commends the Macedonians for doing this (2 Corinthians 8:5). To give yourself means to give your energy, your time, your money, your properties, and your privileges to God—to entrust yourself to Him and have faith that He will supply your needs.

The churches in Macedonia were poor. Out of their severe trial, their extreme poverty and their over-flowing joy they gave generously, freely and cheerfully. Their giving flowed out of their dedication to Christ, their love for their fellow believers and the joy of helping those in need (2 Corinthians 8:1-59). Our greatest example is Jesus Christ, who became poor to enrich us. With all the material and spiritual blessing that God has given us, we can give sacrificially, generously and out of a thankful heart, led by the Holy Spirit.

According to George W. Trimble in his book, *The Gift of Giving*,[1] a good steward must have a godly character and display the following qualities:

♦ *Contentment:* Be satisfied with the provision and security that comes from the Lord (1 Timothy 6:17).

♦ *Patience:* Avoid buying whatever your heart desires when you see it; be willing to save and pay cash for what you need (Galatians 5:22).

- *Self-Control:* Depend on Jesus; spend less than you earn (Galatians 5:22).
- *Discipline:* Look after the resources that God has entrusted to you (1 Chronicles 29:11).
- *Generosity:* Give generously. Generosity demonstrates freedom from slavery to materialism.

Earning

Since God is the creator of the universe, He owns everything in it (Psalm 24:1). The silver and gold belong to God (Haggai 2:8). God gives you the ability to produce wealth and He will supply all your needs (Deuteronomy 8:18). He will also fill you to the measure of all His fullness and the blessings of His presence in your life (Ephesians 3:19-20).

But this does not mean that we sit with our hands folded and wait for God to reward us. The Bible is clear about our need to work and be diligent. The book of Proverbs gives us many wise principles to live by. All hard work brings a profit (Proverbs 14:23). He who works his land will have abundant food. Lazy hands make a man poor, but diligent hands bring wealth (Proverbs 10:4). Through hard and honest work, God moves in the lives of Christians who fully obey Him. Working is the divine principle of giving back to God all that we are and all that we have.

Caroline Adalla, in her book, *Stewardship: Challenging the Church in Africa*,[2] points out that Africa is blessed with good and fertile farm land. If this land is used properly through hard work, it can produce enough food to feed its own people and even other continents. Part of the reason we are hungry is we do not do our best to work the land. Some Christians, especially in rural areas, are blessed with land. Yet most of that land is not used. Sometimes people may not have the right tools or farming knowledge, but in many cases we are lazy. Through diligence we can provide enough food to "lend to many and borrow from none" (Deuteronomy 15:6).

A pastor's wife can use her hands and teach those who are willing to work. Do not give them fish; teach them how to fish. Give them seedlings to plant so that they grow their own vegetables to eat and sell them to get money. By so doing the church and the community will grow mentally, spiritually and financially. The youth of our church were without jobs and just sitting at home. I encouraged them to plant vegetables and sell them. Recently they were able to sell spinach at church to raise funds for the musical instruments they have been wanting.

Another pastor's wife used to give seeds to her church and community to plant on their lands. She helped homes that were starving and families that were sick and unhappy. Because of that she won souls for the Lord and healthy families were built. If you have other talents like sewing, crochet or cake decorating, you can use these skills to beautify your home, provide for your family, and teach others to do the same.

Giving

In the Old Testament God encouraged the Israelites to follow the Law, especially the giving of tithes, by promising to bless them for their obedience. In Genesis 14:20, even before the Law was given, Abraham gave Melchizedek a tenth of all he won from a battle. Melchizedek is called the king of righteousness and king of peace, just like the promised Messiah, showing us that he represented Christ before He came in human form.

Today, we live under New Testament grace, not the Law. Our giving to the Lord is based on our ability to give and our willing heart. Christians today must bring all their tithes and offerings into the house of the Lord. As the children of Abraham, we should give our tithes to the "King of Peace" and the "King of Righteousness"— our Lord and Saviour Jesus Christ. A tithe is one-tenth of our income. We are encouraged to give that, and more.

Tithing and giving are matters of the heart. God always looks on the heart. When you tithe and give just because you are supposed to and not out of love for God, you miss out on the blessings of your giving. In Malachi 1:6-8 the people brought their tithes but were not blessed because of the attitude of the heart. Honour and love were missing from their tithes and offerings. God loves it when you tithe with all your heart and enjoys it when you give Him your best. You should start by giving ten per cent of your income and a hundred per cent of your heart. If a pastor's wife does so, God counts her as one of His special treasures (Malachi 3:16-17).

In 2 Corinthians 9:6-15 Paul encourages the Corinthians to give generously, willingly and cheerfully to the needy saints in Jerusalem. He says this giving is like planting seeds, and the more they plant the more they will reap. What will they reap? A harvest of righteousness and praise to God, as well as many other spiritual blessings. He also tells them they will be made rich in *every way*, so that they can *give even more*.

Adalla offers many biblical principles about giving in her book on stewardship:

- Giving honours God and often results in abundant blessing and provision (Proverbs 3:9-10; Malachi 3:10-11).
- Giving is an act of worship (Matthew 2:11).
- Through our giving we lay up treasures for ourselves in heaven (Matthew 6:19-21).
- Giving with a positive attitude glorifies God (Genesis 4:3-7).
- Giving should be motivated by our love for God and our fellow Christians (2 Corinthians 9:6-7).
- We should give out of a generous heart (1 Chronicles 29:9).
- Our giving should be a cheerful act of grace (2 Corinthians 8:7, 9:7).[3]

Ntokozo was interviewed for a higher position at work, looking forward to the increase in salary. She was certain that she performed well in the interview. Unfortunately she did not get the position. After this incident, she decided to give to God first and then pay her bills. As tithing and giving generously became a habit in her life, God blessed her. She was eventually promoted to a higher position.

As a pastor's wife you should store up for yourself treasure in heaven. The government of heaven has at its head El Shaddai—the One who is more than enough and the One who owns everything. The Philippians gave to Paul's missionary work, and he promised that God would supply all their needs according to His glorious riches in Christ Jesus (Philippians 4:19). You can also deposit into your heavenly account by giving offerings to the work of the gospel, trusting God to supply your needs.

Raise a Giving Church

A giving church is a joyful, growing church. Motivate the church to give. Delegate elders or mature members to teach about giving. If the church is new, and you handle the money, there must be two or three people to witness and help you with your financial records. This will prevent any questions about your integrity or the proper use of the funds. Adalla suggests the following things you can do to raise a giving church:

- Educate the church on the principles of giving and show great interest in the welfare of your members by helping them to identify their talents.
- Designate special tithing Sundays. Motivate members through testimonies of successful givers.
- Read a Scripture on giving before collecting the money.
- Be an example of a good giver—be the first to give.
- Keep proper church records. Every giver wants to know how much money has been contributed. Inform givers of the income and expenditure. Be careful that all money is handled with honesty and in a responsible way (2 Corinthians 8:20-21).
- Beware of using church money for your personal needs if it has not been designated for your salary. Don't allow church members to borrow that money, either. [4]

Saving

Trimble reminds us that if we trust in God as our ultimate source, He will give us wisdom about how to use our money.[5] The Bible encourages us to save. In Proverbs 21:20 we read that in the house of a wise person there are stores of food and oil. Jesus pointed out that it is unwise to begin a long term project without the finances to see it through (Luke 14:28). Saving seems to take time, but Proverbs 28:20 reminds us that a person who wants to get rich quick will only get into trouble.

Saving has several important functions:

- It develops self-discipline in us as we keep our expenses less than our income.

- ❖ It enables us to respond to emergencies.
- ❖ It allows us to pursue dreams such as higher education.
- ❖ It develops a hard-working mind-set in us and teaches us to be careful with money. [6]

Trimble also tells us that although is it wise to save, it is sinful to hoard (Luke 12:16-21). After you have met your needs, if you have extra income, invest it under God's guidance. Some money might be held in the world's system, such as investments and bank savings. This type of investment is not morally wrong. However, if God wants it for His kingdom, then you may have it in the wrong kingdom. The kingdom of God has its own system of investment, the principle of sowing and reaping. God will guide you about where the surplus of income should be used. He will guide you to give to someone in need, which will result in a deposit in your treasure in heaven's account. Do your saving for the glory of the Lord.[7]

The Deception of Debt[8]

There was a man who went to the government offices to apply for his pension. To his shock, he discovered that the computer system said he was dead—he was no longer living on planet earth. His wife, in an effort to pay off some debts she owed, had applied for a death certificate for her own husband in order to cash in on his insurance policies. This caused a very bad situation in the marriage, as you can imagine! Through God's grace, the husband managed to forgive his wife, but their relationship was not like before. Debt and greed caused heartache for this family, and the wife continues to live in debt to this day. She is a Christian, but her life is not a good example to her family, the church or the community.

If you want a healthy and a happy family that is financially secure, keep out of debt. The Bible teaches that we should always repay debts, but since the borrower is slave to the lender (Proverbs 22:7) it is wiser to avoid debt.

If you borrow money you have to pay the lender interest. You end up paying more for the item than if you had saved up until you had enough money to pay cash. This is why you should not buy on credit or enter into a hire-purchase scheme. A hire-purchase scheme is designed to help the seller, not the buyer. You must save and invest your money until you have enough money to buy what you want.

The overuse of credit cards can force a person into debt. It is not wrong to use credit cards, but they should be used as if they were cash that you have in your pocket. Whatever you buy on a credit card should be backed by money in your account, and the bill should be paid at the end of every month.

Going into debt can prevent God from teaching us. God may wish to demonstrate His love for us by providing us with something we want or need, for which we have no resources. If we go into debt, we deny Him that opportunity. He may also be withholding resources because of sin in our lives, or because the item we wish to purchase may not be best for us.

Debt may reveal a spirit of greed in our lives. Jesus warns us not to be greedy for what we do not have. Real life is not measured by how much we own (Luke 12:15). We must realise that all money comes from and really belongs to God. If we understand the difference between needs, wants, and desires, we can avoid running into debt. We must not measure ourselves by the standard of the world. We should be content with what we have. We must be faithful with little before we will be entrusted with much (1 Timothy 6:6-8; Luke 16:10). We should not set our hearts on material wealth but trust God's faithfulness to provide (Philippians 4:19).

Living with debt can create an overwhelming sense of hopelessness, shame and fear. Many people become emotionally paralysed by debt, which can result in physical sickness and mental breakdown. Debt puts huge pressure on people and can cause depression and other negative side effects.

Psalm 37:21 says, "The wicked person borrows and does not repay." Repay debt. Give everyone what you owe to them (Romans 13:7-8). If you have borrowed money you must repay when you have it. To borrow and not repay is wrong and sinful (Proverbs 3:28). It also gives you a bad name. People in the community will begin to know that you are a person who does not repay when you borrow. This could give Christ a bad name as well.

Dealing with debt means accepting responsibility for what you owe and speaking with the creditor with integrity. You must repent before the Lord for the wickedness of not repaying the debt as has been agreed. Trust in the Lord that He will meet all your needs. Let your plans be in line with those of God—then He will solve your problem. When your ways are pleasing to God, He makes your enemies live at peace with you (Proverbs 16:7). If you have creditors who are enemies to you and are not at peace with you, pray and ask God to give you strength to speak to each creditor. Ask them to forgive you for not honouring your word to repay the debt. Make a plan to repay, and honour the agreement from that moment onwards.

Once you have made this agreement you are free from financial and spiritual bondage and God can do wonderful things for you. You may find that resources will begin to flow from unexpected sources.

The Family Budget

We know that God is the source of our provision. He provides our daily bread and various needs. Being a good steward of this provision means planning our expenses with a family budget. The income of the family should be regarded as the income of the whole family and not the private possession of those who receive salaries. A wife who is employed outside the home must share her income with the family. It is not her money to spend as she wishes on new clothes and trips to the salon. If she is not employed outside the home, she is busy creating a loving home and caring for the children. The income her husband earns is as much hers as it is his. Call the family together and draw up a financial plan. The first item is the specific amount for God's work. Then list amounts for all your needs.

If it seems difficult to make a financial plan, you can start by recording all your income and expenditure items under appropriate categories. Do this for two or three months. On the next page is a sample chart from Lean Darwin's Book, *Yes! I'm a Pastor's Wife!*: [9]

At the end of the third month summarise the income and the expenses and determine a monthly average for each item. Does the way you spend your money fit with your priorities? Are you spending more than you have? After making your budget, review it at least once a year and adjust it as needed.

Sample Family Budget

Expenses:	Amount
Tithes & Offerings	
Savings	
Taxes	
Rent	
Electricity	
Phone	
Water	
Cell Phone	
Transportation	
Groceries	
Children's Allowance	
Husband's Allowance	
Wife's Allowance	
Clothing needs	
Ministry Expenses	
Insurance	
School Fees	
Holiday	
Emergencies	
Total Expenses:	
Total Income:	
Less Expenses:	
Deficit or Surplus per month	

Total Expenses:

Income minus total expenses = surplus or deficit.

The Love of Money

Money can be used for either good or evil. We need it. We cannot live life without it. Satan wants us to worship, trust and love money as if it has some power in itself. He wants us to believe that money is an end in itself—even more important than God. The Bible reminds us, "Though your riches increase, do not set your heart on them" (Psalm 62:10b). "For the love of money is a root of all kinds of evil" (1Timothy 6:10a). You cannot serve two masters. You will love and be devoted to the one and hate and despise the other. You cannot serve both God and mammon (Matthew 6:24). God wants us to worship Him alone.[10]

The love of money can make it hard to make godly decisions. A wealthy church member may try to use his wealth to control the pastor or keep him from confronting sin in a church member's life. These days some men and women of God are preaching money. It is taking a lot of time to raise funds in our services, instead of giving the Word the time it deserves.

A pastor was invited to minister at a certain church. Before preaching he ordered the whole congregation to come and greet him, bringing money with them, starting from R200, as a way of shaking his hand. It took two hours to do that and when he preached, the sermon was not based on any Bible passage and there was no theme. These days men and women of God seem to be *selling* the Word instead of *preaching* it (1 Timothy 6:3-5).

You must not forget that the true source of power and provision is God. Therefore you have to decide whether you serve God or mammon. You should never try to use God to get money. If you have a crusade, preach the gospel and don't plan to get money from it.

Adalla tells us of one of the shocking off-shoots of living in poverty and aspiring to rise above the poverty line: Africans who sell their souls to the devil, becoming devil worshippers. Devil worshipping is not a myth. Stories are even told of church leaders who secretly worship the devil in exchange for power and wealth.[11]

The three top areas of downfall for men and women of God are pride, sex and money. We need to be found trustworthy by others and develop integrity in the way we handle money. In 2 Corinthians 8:21 Paul not only acts responsibly before God—that alone is not enough—he also ensures that he is found to be trustworthy among men. To avoid any appearance of corruption, Paul worked alongside his co-workers as well as two others appointed by the church. Paul wanted to do the right thing, not only in the eyes of the Lord but also in the eyes of men. He wanted to be transparent in the accounting of money. If he felt so strongly about this, shouldn't we follow his example as well?

Conclusion

As we talked to different pastors' wives, we met some who had endured times of famine when God did not seem to hear their prayers. There were times when God miraculously supplied their needs. Sometimes He provided generous congregations, times of financial blessing and opportunities to give to others. We could see that God chooses when and how He will bless, and He has His reasons for doing so. Like Paul, we as pastors' wives need to learn "the secret of being content in any and every situation, whether well fed or hungry, whether living in plenty or in want" (Philippians 4:12). We know that we can do everything through Christ who gives us strength (Philippians 4:13).

Your husband may pastor a large church whose wealthy members buy him a car or a new suit every Christmas. That can be a great blessing, but also presents challenges and temptations of its own. For many pastors' wives, however, the challenge will come in the form of continuing to trust God to provide for the family's needs on a limited income. If you are in this situation, take it as an opportunity to stretch your faith, deepen your walk with God, and watch Him bless in ways you never imagined.

Questions to think about and discuss:

1. How do you feel about your family finances? Very secure? Very concerned?

2. How do 1 Chronicles 29:11-12 and Psalm 145:15-19 affect your view of your finances?

3. What can you do to develop a generous heart?

4. How would you rate your financial integrity? What can you and your husband do to be sure you are above reproach when it comes to church finances?

5. Considering Proverbs 22:7, to what degree are you in financial bondage? What steps can you take to get financially free?

6. In your culture, do husband and wife usually have one purse? What are the advantages of a one-purse family?

7. Talk with your husband about developing a family budget based on the sample given.

Discussion questions from this chapter are adapted from *Yes! I'm a Pastor's Wife, 2nd edition*, by Leah Marasigan Darwin (Makati, Philippines: Church Strengthening Ministry, Inc., 2007).

> I don't know anyone in this new church. How will I ever make friends?

> Can a pastor's wife be friends with non-Christians?

> I became close friends with a woman at church. Now the others are jealous. What do I do?

Chapter 9

Friendships Inside and Outside the Church

Khumsa Myrtle Mamane

Every human being needs friends: someone to share emotions and ideas and laugh and cry with—somebody to trust and love. The pastor's wife needs friends more than any other lady alive. With so many daily challenges in ministry, friends to pray with and to share burdens with are greatly needed. But a pastor's wife may feel some degree of loneliness as she serves in her community. Perhaps she is very busy with work, ministry and family. She may be in a new location where the culture is different. She may be the only pastor's wife in her area. She may not feel she can open her heart to the women in her congregation. What can she do to make and keep good friends? Let us understand our friendship journey.

What is Friendship?

Friendship occurs when two or more people like and enjoy each others' company. A friend is somebody who accepts and seeks to know you as you are. A friendship may start from childhood and continue into adulthood. Friends are always happy to see each other after a period of absence. No matter how your friend looks, or how she does things, or the mistakes she makes—you still love her. When adversity hits, the friend offers the desired help and support. In times of sickness, financial stress, or conflicts at work or church, we need friends to comfort us and offer the necessary support. Proverbs 17:17 says, "A friend loves at all times, and a brother is born for adversity." A pastor's wife will have her share of adversity, so a pastor's wife needs friends.

Jesus and His Friends

There is a song, "Friendship with Jesus, fellowship divine. Oh! What blessed sweet communion. Jesus is a friend of mine." This friend, Jesus, loves unconditionally. Jesus is always there to listen to us. We pastors' wives need that type of a friend, a tender compassionate friend. We must first and foremost spend time with our friend, Jesus.

Jesus had His friends—men friends—in the inner circle. Those were His twelve disciples. And he had the three closer friends, Peter, James and John. Of those three, John was "the disciple whom Jesus loved"—his closest friend. He knew them very well. He loved them very much. They were different in character, emotions and skills, but still they bonded together in friendship. He gave them tasks, talked with them, ate and rested with them. He asked them to follow Him.

There were ladies also—Mary, His mother; Mary Magdalene; Martha; and the woman who washed His feet with expensive oil. They cared for Him, thought about Him, knew that he had divine power. Jesus also loved and befriended children. Jesus befriended those who were poor and had afflictions. He still does that today.

Women Need Women

Women enjoy sharing about the everyday aspects of their lives and learning from one another. As a pastor's wife, you need to be free to be the woman you were created to be. Thus you need female friends. With these friends you can chat about diet, make-up, wardrobes, and the arrangement of your lounge. You can exchange recipes, tell each other of sale items in town, and advise each other on sensible ways of keeping within the budget.

As a pastor's wife you must be open-hearted to share friendship with people from many different backgrounds, ages, and lifestyles, both in your community and in your church. But like Jesus, you also need to choose wisely the people you spend much time with. First of all, you need people in your life who can enrich your ministry and who enjoy you and your family. You need friends who will encourage you in times of distress. These friends will be willing to join you in healthy activities like Bible reading, learning new songs and choruses, and prayer. In other words, you need Christian friends.

Friendships with Women in the Church

It is important to be friendly and warm with the other women in your congregation. To have a heart that welcomes others is a vital quality for a pastor's wife. You are imitating Jesus and helping your husband's ministry by the way you relate to others in the church.

One pastor's wife was cold and unfriendly and did not care a bit about her husband's ministry. The husband, a very dedicated pastor, had to see to it himself that his Christian friends and visitors were catered for. However, God still honoured the husband's ministry. A few years ago that lady passed away through a natural cause. The pastor re-married a diligent, loving and warm Christian lady. The ministry is growing in leaps and bounds.

Though you must be open and friendly with everyone in your congregation, beware of sharing prayer items that may be gossip. Be careful what you share about your husband, your children, or anyone for that matter, when that person is not present. It is better to share deep things with a mentor or close friend outside of church whom you can trust to keep things confidential. You may find you can share more deeply with other wives in ministry, since they understand the unique pressures pastors' wives face.

One ministry wife says,

> Sometimes you are at a sinking point in your spiritual life...you need some encouragement or maybe [to] off load. Which is very hard because any brethren you confide in feel exclusively favoured

which normally results in some of the brethren feeling unloved. Thus, you end up burdened and no one to share with. Otherwise, you might risk your laundry being aired in the church billboards.

Wives of your age—peers in other words—can be great as friends. Having children the same age makes child upbringing fun. Three or four of you can have a parent support group even though you've not encountered any problems yet. Have picnics together. Learn games to play with the group. Take along special treats like chocolates, ice cream or fruit for your outings or gatherings. Take time to teach verses or songs each time your group meets. You'll be amazed to find out that the children also develop lifetime friends from that bonding of parents.

Mentors

You also need women in your life from whom you can learn. I've found out that older pastors' wives are good mentors. They've travelled the road before. They are able to share their experiences with younger pastors' wives. I've had two such ladies as my mentors. I enjoy their company. When I visit them I am sure to find some warmth and a great measure of encouragement. Most of the time they detect my area of trouble even before I share the problem. They know me—they can help me always. No matter at what time of the day I knock at their door, they are always there for me. If you have had mentors in your life, ask the Lord to give you some wisdom and strength to be a mentor to others as well.

Neighbours and Workmates

You cannot choose neighbours or workmates. You must accept them as they are. These types of friends are non-Christians in many cases. Go ahead, befriend them. It may not be easy since you do not share the same view of life, but do your level best to make friends with them. They will respect you for who you are—a pastor's wife. Be sure they know that you are a model Christian lady in character. You want them to copy good behavior from you. Do not let them lead you into dishonesty, immorality or other sin. The way you do things will influence their understanding of Christianity. And who knows? They may become Christians one day.

One pastor's wife had a good non-Christian friend. The friend was very loyal and helpful. She would come and help the pastor's wife with household chores. This friend was needy. She had five kids. Her husband had abandoned her. By God's grace the friend was converted. A well-to-do Christian offered a job to this lady. The Lord has been providing for this family in a wonderful way. The kids have accepted the Lord as Saviour, and their friends are joining them. Three of them are already past the tertiary level and are working. The Lord is wonderful.

Find Friends

So how do you acquire friends? Perhaps you are a new pastor's wife and don't know where to start. First of all, remember that to find a friend, you must be a friend. The Bible describes a friend as someone who will lay down her life for another, or someone who sticks closer than a brother. Be observant at church and make an effort to be friendly and kind to people you meet. You hear people testifying at church and learn what they are like. Make it a point to talk to them—visit them if possible. Have a notebook with the people's names and telephone numbers. Call them and chat. Some will respond and keep a link with you. Ask God to bring you friends and to help you see others who are in need of a friend. Invite people to attend social or religious functions with you.

You can make close friendships as you do ministry together. Help each other in evangelizing campaigns. Should there be children's Bible clubs and women's unions, invite others to go along with you. Sometimes women meet together to do handwork. Befriend and show loving care for the poor. Organize clothing and food with your friends and give, give, give. The elderly within our reach may need one or two visits a week—a prayer, a cup of tea or coffee—some nice music on a CD. There are many things that you can do for your elderly friends. Declare the love of God in every situation. The love of Jesus must be known. Souls of non-Christians must be won.

There may be people you know who are not Christians yet. You may not seek them as friends, but they come to you. They come when they need food. They come for company and advice. Perhaps they want to learn some skills from you. They may want to confide in you. Maybe they are hurt--they've met some disappointments in life. Some need jobs. Share their grief. Help them in job hunting. They look upon you as a friend in adversity. Show them the love of God.

Your Family

Our parents, grandparents, and extended family members are friends that we did not have to look for. God just gave them to us. They may or may not be Christians, but they are usually interested in our progress and welfare. They take time to chat with us. We see them at family gatherings every year or so. Let us be thankful to God for our families, showing them our appreciation and love. Let us honour their invitations when they do not clash with our ministry time.

Some family members may be happy that you are a pastor's wife. They become your friends and prayer-partners. On the other hand, some may feel sorry for you that you've married a pastor. Perhaps these family members have even been in the ministry and have met with some disappointments. They have been hungry or met discouragement from other Christian workers. They have been hurt by church board or council members. So, these family members are afraid on your behalf. What if you do not cope? The world is hostile, and you are young. There are a lot of opportunities for you to prosper other than being a pastor's wife. These are threats with some pinch of truth. But—you have been called as a couple to serve the Lord. The one who called you is alive. He is on the throne and ready to supply your needs in spite of your family's fears. So cling to Psalm 37:3-7, 35-36. The Lord is with you no matter what your family says.

Your husband is your most valuable friend. You share everything with him. Your body, mind, and spirit have to blend with his. His likes you must like. His dislikes you must endure. Your pastor spouse needs your warm friendship and support. Friendship starts at home and should grow, drawing more people in, making the circle of friends wider.

How is your relationship with your adult children? When kids grow up they may develop their own opinions and understanding of things. Know that they are not children any longer. Allow them to be themselves, but be their friend and advisor still. They must know that you are always there for them, should they need any type of support. They also know who you are—when you'll say "yes" and when you'll say "no".

Conclusion

There is a saying that friends are easier lost than found. We pastors' wives need to fight against that saying. We need to gather as many friends as possible and not lose them. It takes hard work to make and keep good friends, especially in the ministry. You've got to have a big, loving heart. Owe no one anything except love (Romans 13:8).

There is a story told about a Christian man who came to live in a rural area. He could not speak the language of the people, but he lived among them, loved them, cared for them, and worked with them. Eventually he died and was buried at the edge of the village. Sometime later, some missionaries came who could speak the language of the villagers. They told the people in the village about Jesus and the way He showed compassion to everyone. The villagers replied, "Oh, we have seen him. He came to our village once long ago. He is buried right over there." The whole nature of a person craves the love of God. Our example of love can show people what Jesus is like. By befriending people, our love becomes an arm drawing people nearer to Him.

Questions to think about and discuss:

1. What are the most important qualities of a good friend?

2. Which of the qualities of a good friend do you most need to develop in your own life?

3. What are some of the benefits of being friends with other pastors' wives of your same age?

4. Do you have mentors in your life? What are they like? Are you a mentor to anyone?

5. How can you be good friends with the women in your church and avoid the problems that sometimes come with favouritism?

6. What can you do to develop friendships with non-Christians and open the door to introducing them to your best friend, Jesus?

> If we are all Christians in this church, why do we have so much conflict?

> After what that lady said about me, I don't think I can ever forgive her.

> I'll forgive her, but I won't forget!

Chapter 10

Conflict, Criticism and Forgiveness

Fikile Octavia Mpunzana

A drunken lady was standing in front of the preacher at a crusade, having responded to the invitation to accept Jesus as her Saviour. "How could this woman be born again? She doesn't even know what she is doing!" protested one pastor. The other pastors disagreed with him. "Who are you to argue with the work of the Holy Spirit in someone's life?" Conflict came into the crusade and threatened to cause division. Fortunately, the lady testified later when she was sober that she had indeed been saved. The pastors were able to deal with their differences and fellowship was restored.

Satan wants to take every opportunity to use conflict to destroy the work of God. As a pastor's wife, you will find that there is often conflict in the church—and you will sometimes be at the centre of it! The principles in this chapter have helped me, and I hope they will help you as well. You can learn to manage conflict and criticism, and to forgive completely from your heart. You will find as a pastor's wife that others will look to you for guidance when they have conflicts. These principles can also help you to help others solve their problems—in families, in churches and in the community.

A Biblical View of Conflict

Ken Sande, in his book, *The Peacemaker*, defines conflict as a difference in opinion that frustrates someone's goal or desires.[1] Leah Darwin calls it friction, disharmony or discord caused by differences in opinion, in world views and in personalities. Whenever there is more than one person involved in any activity or group there is sure to be conflict.[2]

Not all conflict is bad. Each and every person is unique, so we have different opinions. These differences can help us to exercise our minds and grow in solving problems together. We need to remember that we are all are made in God's image and every human being is worthy of honour and respect. As a pastor's wife you should learn to accept and work with people who see things differently than you do. You are in Christ, and in Him are hidden all the treasures of wisdom and knowledge (Colossians 2:3). This knowledge will enable you to value all types of people. Paul encourages us to accept everyone as Christ has accepted us, and when we do this, we bring praise to God (Romans 15:7).

While conflicts may begin because of our different ways of looking at things, they become worse because of our sinful reactions. In fact, many conflicts *start* because of sinful actions and desires. Jesus tells us that this evil comes from our heart (Mark 7:20-23). James also reminds us that conflict starts in our heart (James 4:1-2). Jeremiah 17:9 says, "The heart is deceitful above all things and beyond cure." Even though we are Christians these verses are still talking to us. As long as we are living, our sinful nature lives in us together with our new nature. These two natures fight within us. I need to decide which side I will feed. I can feed my new nature with the Word of God, or feed my old nature by saturating it with things of this world.

How can I live with this fight within me? By daily confessing my sin (1 John 1:9) and by being delivered from the power of sin. Romans 6:11-18 tells us to consider ourselves dead to sin and to offer our bodies as slaves to righteousness. By confessing, meditating on the Word of God, and living a prayerful life, I can feed the new nature and avoid many conflicts.[3]

Sande tells us that conflict is an opportunity to demonstrate the presence and power of God. In the middle of a conflict, you can take the opportunity to glorify God, to serve others and grow to be like Christ.

When you find yourself in a conflict, ask yourself; *"How can I please and honour God in this situation?"* The best way to glorify God is to follow His Word and obey His commands. If I handle my conflict in a godly way, that will glorify Christ and people will be drawn to Him (Matthew 5:16; John 17:4). Too often people are driven away from Christ because of conflicts between church members. As a pastor's wife, imitate Christ by loving your enemies—leave the rest to God (Luke 6:27-36). Ask Him to give you strength to help those who hate you. Try to the best of your ability to listen to their point of view and pray for them. By focusing on trusting, obeying and imitating God, your feet will not slip (Psalm 37:31).

Another question to ask is, *"How can I serve others in this situation?"* Jesus says that you must love your enemies and do good to those who hate and mistreat you. You must help your opponents and encourage them to trust in the Lord. If you handle disputes in a godly manner, this will teach and encourage others in similar situations. When it is difficult to love and serve our enemies, we must remember how much we love Christ and how He loves us. This will give us courage and help us to serve our enemies wholeheartedly.

A certain pastor didn't get his stipend for eight months. It was not easy to continue loving the church members in this situation. He was worried about the bills and school fees that could not be paid. His wife encouraged him to serve the Lord with all his heart even though the church did not give him his stipend. He continued to visit the members in their homes, prayed for the sick and took care of the widows and orphans. As the pastor served his church and community, God touched other people—friends, relatives, and believers from other churches—to support him. Eventually his church learned to support him as well.

When you are in the middle of a conflict, it can be painful. But *God can use conflict to develop you to be more like Christ.* God's highest purpose for you is to conform you to the image of His Son (Romans 8:29). Conflict can challenge you, causing you to depend and trust more on God, making you more like Jesus. To be like Christ means to do things like Christ, to speak and act like Him. When people hurt you, show them love and forgiveness like Jesus did. (Luke 23:34). Take conflict as a stepping stone to growth rather than trying to avoid it. Conflict becomes a blessing as God uses it in your life to make you more like Jesus.

A steward is like a manager who is entrusted by a company to look after a business. The manager is expected to be faithful in following the company's instructions for the good of the company, not himself. When you are in a conflict, God is trusting you to solve the conflict in a godly manner, using wisdom from His Word and the strength of the Holy Spirit, as well as the skills and abilities he has given you (Luke 12:42).

To manage your conflict effectively you need to understand your Master's will in the situation. Don't forget that you are not alone—you have the Holy Spirit to give you the strength and power to do the right thing, and you can call upon mature Christians to help you as well. Most of all, you must be faithful to resolve the conflict in a way that pleases God (1 Corinthians 4:2). Then you will hear His "Well done, good and faithful servant!" (Matthew 25:21a).

Criticism

Pastors and their wives often face criticism from the congregation or from the community. Sometimes criticism can be helpful. Usually it is painful, especially if it comes from an immature person with wrong motives. It is hard to receive criticism from the very people you are trying to serve and love. As a new pastor's wife, you may encounter criticism because you are not yet used to the ministry. It is not easy to take, and you may not be sure how to respond. Understand that you are facing many new things, and just stick to the Word of God for comfort and guidance. Most of these criticisms you can overlook and forgive. Know that God will help you grow through what you are facing.

Pastor Mncwabe and his wife served a church that had been deserted by many pastors because of its behaviour. This pastor's wife devoted herself to prayer and fasting and invited others to join her in prayer. Through prayer and perseverance God helped this couple. The church grew and its behaviour changed. However, some members in the church were not happy with this pastor's wife because she was not from their area. They began to say that the pastor's wife was using magic to manipulate and draw people to come to church. She and her husband lived in a house with a wooden floor, and snakes used to get under the house. So these church members spread rumours that she was using snakes to bewitch and manipulate her husband and to gain more respect in her position as the pastor's wife. Others looked down on her, telling her that she had no profession, was uneducated, and was not a suitable partner for her husband. Instead of praising God for what He was doing in the church, they criticised her. Yet she served the Lord wholeheartedly in spite of all the discouragements she encountered.

How does God want us to respond to criticism? First of all, *know who you are*. Remember that you are a child of God and a joint heir with Jesus (Romans 8:16-17). God has totally accepted you, and that is more important than anyone's opinion.

Be filled with the Holy Spirit (Ephesians 5:18). This means you need to allow God to develop Christ's character in you and follow Jesus' example. Jesus Christ was attacked and criticised. He responded by being meek and lowly in heart. When we face such times, Jesus wants us to come to Him and find rest for our souls (Matthew 11:28-29). When we are criticised we are tempted to become angry and sour. We want to make sure that the attacker knows she is wrong. Leah Darwin reminds us that meekness would stop us and make us go to God, asking Him to soften our hearts and decrease our anger.[4]

It is not easy to respond in this way, especially if it is your husband being attacked. You may want to defend him to other people in the church. Although sometimes it may be necessary to explain a situation so the truth can be known, I have found that usually the best thing is to keep quiet, knowing that one day God will reveal the truth.

It is also important to *have a forgiving heart*. We are commanded to forgive as God in Christ forgave us. Thoko didn't wear expensive clothes. Sometimes people would make fun of her, asking "Where do you buy your clothes?" Through God's grace she didn't allow those people to burn her up, but she overlooked their comments and forgave them. Jesus forgave his enemies on the cross, and we need to follow His example.

Take time to *examine yourself* with the help of the Holy Spirit (Psalm 139: 23-24). Dale Carnegie suggests that we should not wait for our enemies to criticise us—we should beat them to it. We must tell ourselves, "If my critics had known about all my other faults, they would have criticised me much more severely than they did." Carnegie tells the story of a door-to-door soap salesman who was about to lose his job because of poor sales. He decided to go back to all his customers—not to sell them soap, but to ask for their advice and criticism. This attitude won him a lot of friends and good advice. Because of that, he rose to become the president of the Colgate-Palmolive-Peet soap company.[5]

Sometimes as pastor's wives we deserve the criticism we receive. Are we gossiping about church members, distorting the truth, failing to keep our promises? Do we refuse to involve ourselves in the church, telling the members that we are not "called" as our husbands are? Ask God to show you if you have any of these attitudes (1 Corinthians 13:5) and ask the Holy Spirit to help you change. We can always learn from criticism, even if it is given in the wrong spirit. The Holy Spirit can guide us into all truth. He can help us sift through the bad and keep the good. We need to regularly ask spiritually mature Christians for helpful criticism and thank them for it.

Sometimes you may be criticised for being obedient to God's Word. We are very firm about worshipping God alone, and we don't allow anyone in our church to worship their ancestors. We receive criticism for that, but we just stick to the Word of God and don't change.

Dale Carnegie gives us three practical rules in his book, *How to Stop Worrying and Start Living*, which can keep you from worrying about criticism.

Rule 1: Realise that unjust criticism is often a disguised compliment. It may mean that you have aroused jealousy and envy in others who are not happy about your success.

Rule 2: Do the very best you can and then put up your old umbrella and keep the rain of criticism from running down the back of your neck. In other words, don't let the criticism discourage you.

Rule 3: Keep a record of the foolish things you have done and criticise yourself. Since you can't hope to be perfect, ask for unbiased, helpful criticism from others as well.[6]

Leah Darwin, in her book, *Yes! I'm a Pastor's Wife!*, reminds us that as pastors' wives, we are leaders and role models. We must respond to criticism in a godly way. Peter tells us to shepherd our flock, serving them freely and lovingly the way Jesus, the Good Shepherd did (1 Peter 5:1-4). You can't do that alone. Walk with God in humility, asking God to flood your soul with the gentleness of Christ. Let God take care of your image and reputation, and in so doing you will become more like Christ.[7]

Confessing Our Sin

When we are facing conflict or criticism, it is easy to focus on the person who is causing us grief. But the Bible teaches us to first focus on God, and then to focus on ourselves. Is it possible that our actions or attitudes have caused the conflict or are making it worse? When the Holy Spirit shows us our part in a conflict, we need to be ready to go to the person and confess our sin. Jesus tells us to get the log out of our own eye before we go to show our brother or sister their fault (Matthew 7:5). Usually simply saying sorry isn't enough. We need to think carefully about our sin and its effects on the other people involved. We need to understand how our sin affects our relationship with God as well. We need to be willing to change.

A certain pastor used to go alone to crusades and was led into the temptation of having affairs. When his wife asked him about it he confessed that it was true, but he kept on doing it. This deeply offended her. Eventually that man of God decided to alter his behaviour. He took his wife and went to the senior pastor to confess specifically about his behaviour and admit that he had failed to be the kind of husband God wanted him to be. He decided to raise more funds so that his wife could travel with him in the ministry. They worked on their relationship together, learning to respect and love each other once again. His repentance was shown by his actions and attitudes towards his wife.

Ken Sande, in his book, *The Peacemaker*, gives several aspects of a sincere confession. A person who is truly sorry for her sin will begin by *confessing to God*, knowing that all sin is first against Him (Psalm 51:4). Then she needs to *confess to the person* or people involved, being sure not to talk to more people than necessary. When you confess to someone, *avoid* the temptation to shift the blame to others or to excuse your guilt. Adam and Eve were the first to do this when God confronted them about their sin (Genesis 3:12-13). *Admit* that what you did violated God's will. The prodigal son said to his father, "I have sinned against heaven and against you" (Luke 15:21). There was no "but" or "perhaps" in his confession. *Apologise* for hurting another person's feelings. Show that you understand the pain your actions or words have caused. *Accept the consequences* of your actions. The prodigal son was willing to become a hired servant in his father's house (Luke 15:19). Explain to the person offended how you will *alter* your behaviour in the future. The pastor in the story above made a plan to prevent future temptation by always travelling with his wife. Realise that even with a sincere confession, the person may not be ready to forgive you. Allow time for hurts to heal and trust to be rebuilt.

A pastor's wife should be the first to confess her faults in a conflict. Jesus commanded us to go and sort things out with our brother or sister before bringing our gifts to the altar (Matthew 5:23-24). Our worship and fellowship with God will be restored when we confess our sin. So, if God is showing you some sin in your life, don't delay to confess it. In this way, you will be a good example to others and stay in fellowship with your Saviour. You will glorify God, serve others, and grow to be like Christ. Freedom from sin is good news. The Bible calls a forgiven person "blessed" (Psalm 32:1-5).

Offering Forgiveness

We were neither righteous nor good when Christ died for us—we were sinners. God gave us His gift of love by forgiving us. Therefore, we Christians should forgive other people in the same way we have been forgiven. Paul reminds us to "bear with each other and forgive whatever grievances you may have against one another. Forgive as the Lord forgave you" (Colossians 3:13). In the Lord's Prayer, Jesus taught us to ask God to forgive us in the same way we have forgiven others (Matthew 6:12). Sometimes we do forgive other people, but we find that it is not easy to become friendly with those people again. We struggle to forgive the way God has forgiven us.

Two women in the church were involved in conflict. They were both involved in the leadership of the women's meetings and could not agree who should be in charge. The pastor's wife sat down with them and counselled them to help solve the problem. They forgave each other, but one of them told her friends, "I forgave her verbally, but I will not forget what she did to me!" The outcome was that she held a grudge against her opponent. She even became bitter in the church. She failed to replace her words of hatred and anger with the Word of God. Is that truly forgiveness?

Forgiveness is not a *feeling*. H. Norman Wright says it is a clear and logical action on your part.[8] It is not an emotional response—it is an act of the will. You don't forgive just because you feel like forgiving. You have to decide not to allow the pain of the past to become a permanent crutch in your life, regardless of your feelings.

Forgiveness is not *forgetting*. God constructed you in such a way that your brain is like a computer. Anything that happened to you is stored in your memory. The remembrance will always be with you. You may recall the offense in such a way that it continues to affect you and your relationship with another, or you may remember that it did happen but it no longer hurts you or makes you angry. The best way is to imitate God by choosing not to think, mention or talk about your offender. We may recall the incident, but not with feelings of anger or vengeance.

Forgiveness is not *pretending*. You cannot ignore the fact that an event occurred. Wishing it never happened will not erase it. If you fail to confront and reconcile with the other person, you encourage her to repeat the same behaviour.

Forgiveness is not *bringing up the past*. It is easy to bring up past offenses. In fact there is nothing you can do to change a past event. Even if you were severely hurt, by dwelling on the offense you place a burden on your relationship. This behaviour also denies the presence and power of the person of Jesus Christ in your life.

Forgiveness is not *excusing*. Excusing says, "What you did really wasn't wrong" or "You couldn't help it." Forgiveness is the opposite of excusing. Forgiveness says, "We both know that what you did was wrong and without excuse, but since God has forgiven me—I forgive you." Forgiveness brings a freedom that no amount of excusing could ever provide.

Aphiemi is a Greek word often translated "forgiveness" in the Bible. It means to let go or release. It refers to debts that have been cancelled or paid in full.[9] This is the word Jesus uses in the Lord's Prayer and in the parable of the unforgiving servant (Matthew 6:12; 18:27, 32). Forgiveness is undeserved and cannot be earned (Luke 7:42-43). When you cancel a debt it means that you will pay it yourself, even though the other person deserves to pay. When you forgive you deliberately accept the hurts and pains of life and drop all the charges against your offender. This is what Jesus did for us on the cross when He took on Himself the full penalty of our sins (Isaiah 53:4-6). This is what God is asking us to do when we forgive others.

When you forgive, you give love and freedom where the offender deserves punishment. Fran and Les Hewitt, in their book, *The Power of Focus for Women*, say "To forgive the unforgiveable is the highest form of love. In return you will be blessed with peace and compassion." [10]

When we offer forgiveness to someone, the kind of forgiveness God offers us, Ken Sande says we are making four promises:

1. I will not think about this incident (Jeremiah 31:34).
2. I will not bring up this incident again and use it against you (1 Corinthians 13:5).
3. I will not talk to others about this incident (Proverbs 26:20).
4. I will not allow this incident to stand between us or hinder our personal relationship (Luke 6:27-28, Matthew 5:24b).

By making these promises we tear down the walls that stand between us and the one who offended us.[11] We are accepting the offender when both of us know he or she severely hurt us. It is easier to forgive when we remember that we too are sinners in need of forgiveness (1 John 1:8). God has forgiven us so much—how can we refuse to forgive our brothers and sisters? (Ephesians 4:32) Forgiveness gets us free of the bondage of the sins of disobedience and bitterness. As we release the anger inside us, we can draw closer to God and to our brothers and sisters in Christ.

We should break the wall of anger that separates us from God and the one who hurt us. There are spiritual and emotional scars that need healing. The Bible calls this *reconciliation—a process involving a change of attitude that leads to a change of relationship.*[12] Paul says that we should be transformed by the renewing of our mind. Reconcile with your offender and work hard for a good relationship, replacing bad thoughts, critical words, and unkind deeds with positive ones (Philippians 4:4-7, 2 Corinthians 2:7).

Behave as if you loved that person, and you will come to love them. The Holy Spirit taught me to love someone who hurt me by reading and meditating on the Greatest Commandment—to love God with all my heart and love my neighbour as myself (Mark 12:30-31). In my church there was a boy who didn't want to greet me, and it hurt me. One day I decided to greet him whether or not he responded. After doing it a few days, that resentment melted away and the gap between us was closed. Now it is as if nothing ever happened.

You can *forgive* from your heart, but there may be some cases where it is not easy to *reconcile*—to restore the relationship—if the person has not repented. If a person was physically abusive to you and has not repented, it would not be wise or safe to approach the person to reconcile. Wait until they have shown evidence of true sorrow and a change of behaviour. Allow time for them to show they are trustworthy before trying to reconcile.

When Should We Forgive?

In our daily life, sometimes people commit minor offenses against us. Proverbs 19:11 says it is better to overlook these offenses, even if the person has not repented. You can decide to forgive the offender, knowing that is it your responsibility to heal yourself. Unforgiveness saps your energy. Some illnesses can be linked to holding on to anger and resentment.[13]

When an offense is serious you need to approach the person, show him his fault, and give him a chance to repent (Matthew 18:16-20). You make a decision not to dwell on the painful event. You take time to pray for the offender and reconcile with him as soon as he does repent. Then close the matter forever, the same way that God forgives you.

The Majola family's son disappeared and was found dead a short time later. No one knew who the murderer was. After two years the murderer got saved. He confessed to the police that he had killed the Majolas' son. The police accepted his testimony and released him. Later he returned to the police station and asked them to put him in jail, because he deserved the punishment. The murdered son's parents forgave the murderer unconditionally. The people in the community didn't believe the parents could really forgive him, nor did the offender. Yet they were able to stay with him peacefully. That step of forgiveness protected them from bitterness and resentment and was a testimony to the community.

What About Consequences?

Sometimes forgiveness does not remove the consequences of sin. In 2 Samuel 11 David stole Uriah's wife and made a plot to kill Uriah. After Uriah's death David repented. God forgave him, but he lost his son. When God forgives us, He quickly removes the penalty of separation from Him and spares us from many of the consequences of our sins. But when God allows certain consequences to remain for a time, it is to teach us and others not to sin again. In David's case, David wrote Psalm 51, teaching us a prayer of forgiveness and cleansing.

Ntombi was known as an honest treasurer in her church. However, when her books were checked by an outside auditor it was discovered that a certain amount had disappeared. She confessed that she had used that money for herself and asked the church to forgive her. She was forgiven, but she still had to repay that money.

There are times when you are willing to forgive someone, but you cannot afford to pay the consequences of their sin yourself. Then you must make a plan with the person to restore what was lost. Sometimes you are able to absorb the cost, but if the person is irresponsible, it would not be wise to do so. They must learn to make better choices by feeling the consequences of their sin (Prov. 19:19). Otherwise, they will never change.

Bitterness and Unforgiveness

In Hebrews 12:15, the Bible talks about the root of bitterness:

> See to it that no one misses the grace of God and that no bitter root grows up to cause trouble and defile many.

A root is the underground path for nourishment for a tree or plant. For us as people, our roots are those habitual ways we drink and get our nurture from God, ourselves or others. But if we have roots of bitterness, we will be drinking harm, not good for ourselves. This will produce fruit, but the kind of fruit we don't want in our lives—fruit that is destructive to ourselves and defiles others. Bitter roots come from allowing sinful reactions and negative attitudes to take a foothold in our hearts, making condemning judgements of people, and refusing to forgive others. Bitter roots are not the hurtful or terrible things that happen to us, nor are they the sins of those who wronged us. They are our sins.

In Mark 11:13 Jesus Christ cursed a fig tree. The fig tree dried up from the roots. You can cut a tree down, but if the roots have life, the tree will grow again. Many pastors' wives have failed to deal with the roots of bitterness in their lives. As a result, they have hurt themselves and caused trouble in the church.

A pastor and his wife found themselves facing a group of angry young people from the church. This group was passing remarks, throwing insults at them and telling them to leave the mission house. The couple was shocked because there had been no outward sign of hatred among these young people. But the root of bitterness had grown up in the lives of these young people, and it burst out on that day, defiling many people in the church and community. Through God's grace the pastor and his wife continued to minister to the church with love, and some young people repented of their bitter attitudes. God helped this couple to remain faithful and to win many souls both in the church and the community.

In the ministry, it can happen that we are misunderstood and hurt by others. This can lead to bitterness. How can we deal with the root of this bitterness?

- Ask the Lord to show you any possible bitter roots or judgemental attitudes in your
- relationships.
- See how these bitter roots have defiled your life and others people's lives.

- Confess and repent.
- Forgive from your heart.
- Say: "I renounce the bitter roots that I have planted as a result of hatred and my judgements. In Jesus name I break the power of the hatred, judgements and bitter roots over myself and others."[14]

If we are having a hard time forgiving someone, it may be that we believe that the offender doesn't deserve our forgiveness. We want to punish the offender and make them suffer, and we want a guarantee that such an offense will never happen again. We need to remember that we don't deserve God's forgiveness either. While we were still sinners, Christ died for us (Romans 5:8). Just as God demands no guarantee from us regarding our future conduct, we have no right to make such a demand of others (Luke 17:3-4).

To overcome unforgiveness we need to focus on how God has forgiven us. We behave as if others' sins against us are more serious than our sins against God. We need to repent from this sinful attitude. As pastors' wives we must forgive each time our opponent asks for forgiveness. We have no right to hoard it. Jesus said to his disciples that they must forgive no matter how many times their brother sins and repents. They were amazed at God's standard of forgiveness (Luke 17:3-4).

In Matthew 18:21-35 a servant owed the king an enormous debt. The king cancelled the debt of the servant but that servant then refused to give time to a man who owed him a small debt. The king heard about this and threw him over to the jailers to be tortured. The king called him a "wicked servant". It was because of wickedness that he couldn't forgive and be patient with his fellow servant. His own debt had been cancelled. He should have cancelled the other man's debt and forgiven him for not repaying it.

God wants us to forgive others from our heart. If we forgive from our hearts there will be no root of bitterness. In Matthew 17:3-4 it says that if your brother sins, rebuke him and if he repents, forgive him. Even if he sins against you seven times in a day, and seven times comes back to you and says "I repent," forgive him. True forgiveness depends on God's grace. If you rely on God's strength you can forgive even the most painful offenses. God gives you His strength through the Scriptures and through the Holy Spirit.[15]

Conclusion

At times conflict can push you beyond your limits. It can frustrate you, and you may have a difficult time understanding how to respond to a particular situation. As a pastor's wife, be that kind of a wife whose husband will turn to her for encouragement, biblical advice and support. Support his efforts to be faithful to God. You can help your husband to resolve many conflicts that would defeat him. Through you, God will be glorified.

T. D. Jakes, in his book, *The Lady, Her Lover and Her Lord*, [16] encourages you to be a woman of integrity and be constant in your love. You must not be moved by other people's opinions or ideals. You are the harbour where all types of people dock their fears and find shelter in the storms of life. You are the refuge to which they run. If you believe in what you are, you will stand against the winds of adversity.

As a child of God, you have wisdom and knowledge in Christ. You have what you need to manage conflict faithfully. God has put within us faithfulness—a supernatural strength to keep going when things get tough, to forgive other people, and to rebuild relationships with people who have offended us.

As a pastor's wife, you have no choice but to forgive and reconcile with people who have deeply hurt you. As you imitate the forgiveness and reconciliation that was demonstrated on the cross, you will show others that it is possible, through God's grace, to forgive as the Lord forgave you.

Questions to think about and discuss:

1. Where do all conflicts begin, according to James 4:1-3?

2. How can conflict be an opportunity to glorify God and serve others?

3. Have you ever been criticised by another person? How did you handle it?

4. What is forgiveness? Why is it so important?

5. Have you ever allowed a bitter root to grow in your heart? How did you deal with it?

6. As a pastor's wife, what character qualities do you need to develop to best handle criticism of yourself or your husband?

7. Describe a recent conflict in your church or family. If the principles in this chapter had been followed, how would it have turned out differently?

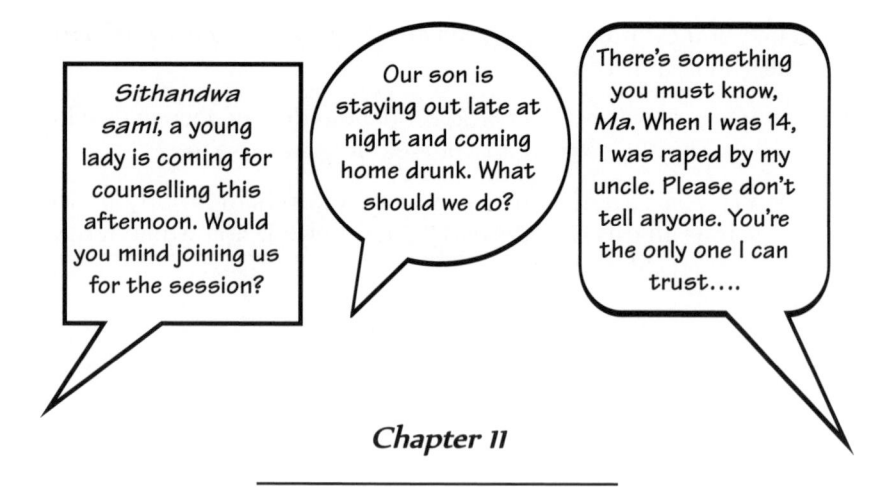

> *Sithandwa sami*, a young lady is coming for counselling this afternoon. Would you mind joining us for the session?

> Our son is staying out late at night and coming home drunk. What should we do?

> There's something you must know, *Ma*. When I was 14, I was raped by my uncle. Please don't tell anyone. You're the only one I can trust....

Chapter 11

Basic Counselling Skills

Susan Binion

Whether you are visiting after a Sunday morning service, or sipping a cup of tea with a friend, or chatting over the fence as you hang out your washing, everyday life presents many opportunities to offer counsel and advice to others. Because you are married to the pastor, others will see you as a leader and a person who can be trusted. You will find many people bringing their problems to you and sharing their hearts. How will you respond?

You may also find it is a help to your husband to have a woman present when he is counselling other women. There are also many problems that women face that may call for the insight that only another woman can give. In the case of rape or domestic abuse, a woman might be afraid to speak to a man. So there are many reasons to improve your counselling skills.

What are the qualities of a good counsellor?

First of all, a counsellor must have *a vital, growing, relationship with*

God, spending time with Him in prayer and in His Word every day. Knowing the Bible well, and having a heart that is willing to obey it, is the way to grow in wisdom. The fear of the Lord is the beginning of wisdom (Proverbs 1:7). The Bible holds much truth for daily living, and the Holy Spirit gives us the power to understand it and do what it says. When we counsel people, we want to offer truth that has made a difference in our own life.

A counsellor also needs to be *sincerely interested in people* and have a warm and welcoming personality. This means that we accept people as they are, with all of their problems, and love them. We are empathetic; that is, we can understand the difficulties the person is facing and the pain they may be feeling.

A counsellor is a *patient listener*. We allow the other person to open her heart without interrupting her. We are not judgmental. We don't try to jump in and solve the problem quickly, offering many Bible verses to fix everything before the person has had a chance to share all they wanted to say.

A counsellor also is able to *keep confidences*. Unless the person is threatening to harm herself or someone else, there is usually not a need to tell anyone else what is shared in the counselling session. This builds trust with the person you are counselling and helps them to open up more.

A counsellor must herself be *emotionally healthy*. This doesn't mean that you never have problems, but that you have an inner strength to adjust to the difficult situations you may face. It means that you are willing to take responsibility for your actions, and that you accept yourself as God has made you. You have healthy relationships with the important people in your life, and you know how to forgive and be forgiven.[1]

What are some of the goals of counselling?

1. To win the *confidence* of the person so that she will be willing to continue the relationship and get the help she needs.
2. To help the person believe that *God's love and power are sufficient* to accept, heal, forgive and help her. To give her *hope* that change is possible.

3. To help the person understand and face the *true nature of her problem*.
4. To help the person *see the need to make wise and godly life choices* that will bring permanent change in her life.
5. To help the person to *grow in her relationship with Christ* and to become more like Him by obeying God's Word.
6. To help the person develop to the point that she is *independent* of you, the counsellor, and can apply what she has learned to new situations on her own. [2]

What should happen in a counselling session?

Some counselling sessions happen naturally as you converse with friends or people in the church. At other times, someone may approach you and ask to meet together to discuss a certain issue. In either case, there are things that should take place to ensure a positive outcome for your time together.[3]

1. **Prepare yourself and the place.** Offer your own distracted thoughts and busy day to God and pray that Christ may be seen and felt in you. Make sure there will be no interruptions with the phone, television, or other people.
2. **Set the person at ease.** Help the person to feel accepted and welcomed. Show your sincere interest in her and your desire to help her.
3. **Gather information and identify problems.** Take time to discover why the person is troubled, and how she views her situation. Listen well and ask questions when appropriate. As she talks out her problem, she will get greater insight into the situation. She may come to understand some of the reasons for her problems and what can be done about them.
4. **Apply Scripture appropriately.** When the time is right, help the person to see her problem from God's point of view. Scripture can guide, challenge, convict, and bring repentance and hope.
5. **Develop a plan of action.** The person you are counselling needs to be brought to a place of planning a course of action, to move

in a certain direction, to begin to solve the problem. Based on Scripture and with the help of the Holy Spirit, help the person identify steps she could take to change her situation. If she is born again, she has new life in her heart, and through the power of the Holy Spirit change is possible.

6. **Assign homework.** Often the person being counselled needs time to think about what you have been discussing, to consider scriptures, and to pray about the next step. Sometimes she may need input from a book or DVD that you recommend. Perhaps she is trying to break a habit, and you ask her to keep track of her progress. These are all examples of homework you may give to the person being counselled.

7. **Pray.** Prayer is expressing our dependence on God. No matter what the situation is, praying with and for the person you are counselling is essential to her growth and healing.

Listening Skills

The most important skill a counsellor must have is the ability to listen well. In fact, listening can be a ministry in itself. We can communicate our concern for the other person by listening to her story without interrupting, jumping to conclusions, judging or arguing. We are often tempted to preach and quickly fix another person's problems before we have really heard what they have to say. If we give advice or start to tell our own story, we may discourage them from sharing their whole heart. Listening well will show the person that we love and respect them and will keep the door open for future conversations.

When listening to someone, listen to the whole person, not just her words. Things like her tone of voice, how fast she is talking, the feelings behind her words, her body language, and even her silences can help you understand what she is trying to say. Don't interrupt or ask too many questions, but allow the story to flow out naturally. When the person you are counselling has finished her story, Christian Listeners-KZN suggest three questions you can ask her to help her think about what she has told you.

1. What do you think is of *most importance* in what you have been saying?
2. Is there anything you would like to *do* about it?
3. What are you *feeling* at this moment about what you have just shared?[4]

There are different ways to show the person that you are listening carefully. You can ask questions to *clarify* what the person has said and help her to look at all sides of the issue. You can *restate* what the person has said in another way to show you understand and are listening well. Occasionally saying something *neutral* like "I see" or "I understand" can encourage the person to keep talking. You can simply *reflect* back to the person what she has said and identify the emotions related to her story. Always take time to *summarise* what the person has said to make sure you understand the main issues, or to shift the conversation in a new direction.[5]

For some people, to be heard is all they need. Others will welcome your advice and suggestions. In some cases, you may not feel qualified to help them with their problem, and must be ready to refer them to others who have the expertise that is needed. Always ask if you can pray for them at the end of your time together. Remember that you don't need to have all the answers, because by listening well you can often help the person find their own solutions to their problems.

What are some of the special situations I may encounter as I counsel women in my church?

Marriage and family life

A pastor's wife has the privilege of entering into the lives of the people in her church, experiencing both their joys and their sorrows. From assisting your husband with pre-marital counselling to offering advice to a brand-new mother, you may have many opportunities to counsel women with God's perspective in these areas. Take time to learn what the Bible says about these important issues. Visit your local Christian bookstore to find books with practical advice for mothers and wives. Become an expert, not only in your head knowledge, but in your own obedience to God's word. Make sure that you are becoming the wife and mother God wants you to be.

Personal conflicts

Much of life's sorrow comes from our failure to live at peace with others, whether they are people in our family, church or community. As a pastor's wife, you may listen to many heartbreaking stories of failed relationships and their painful consequences. Again, you must be very familiar with what the Bible says about these issues, and be an example in your church of a gracious person who willingly confesses her own faults and forgives others (see Chapter 10).

Bereavement and loss

When a person loses a loved one or suffers some other kind of major loss in her life, she needs someone to walk with her through the valley she is experiencing. It is helpful to understand the path that most people take as they go through loss and how to help them at each step of the way. People usually go through five basic stages as they face loss.[6]

1. **Denial:** *"It can't be!"* In the shock of first hearing bad news, a person usually denies that it is happening. This is a normal response. At this point, the counsellor must listen, listen, listen. Encourage the person to talk. Be patient, compassionate, and accepting.

2. **Anger:** *"It's not fair! Why me? It's someone else's fault!"* A person may express anger toward God, themselves, the person who caused the pain, or even the counsellor. She may feel guilty underneath her anger and need to understand God's forgiveness of herself and others. She may go back and forth between denial and anger. Again, the counsellor must listen, and not judge. Ask the person questions to help her understand if her anger is valid. Don't argue with her, but try to get her to put her feelings into words. Allow time for her emotions to become more stable before trying to reason with her.

3. **Bargaining:** *"If God would only _____, I promise I will never _____ again."* At this point, the person is looking for a way out of the situation. Listen and accept what she says. Try to help her think about her bargaining with questions like, "Will that really help? How does that affect the situation?"
4. **Depression:** *"It's hopeless."* The person is now feeling the full weight of the loss she is experiencing. She must go through this stage to find wholeness. Walk closely with her during this time. Keep listening. It doesn't help to tell the person to "get over it." Time is needed to come to a place of acceptance and hope.
5. **Acceptance:** The person has now begun to accept the loss and move on with life. She is at peace with the situation and is able to function normally again. She may find she has grown personally and in her relationship with God as a result of what she has experienced.

Rape

Rape is sometimes defined as a crime of violence using sex as a weapon. If a woman comes to you immediately following a rape, it is important to get her to a hospital for medical help. She must not wash herself until the doctor has examined her for proof of the rape. Then she will have the choice to open a case with the police, if she wants to. At the hospital, she will also be given medicine to help prevent HIV infection if she is HIV negative. Over the following weeks and months, she will likely go through the stages of grief as she faces the emotional pain and physical violation she endured.

If the rape occurred some time ago and she is just getting the courage to talk about it now, you will need to listen as she re-lives the event and walks through the pain she experienced. In both cases, encourage her to cry out to God through prayer and by reading the Psalms. She can express herself through poems or artwork. Although anger is a natural response, bitterness will eventually cripple a person. So at the right time, encourage her to forgive the one who raped her. A woman who is raped feels violated and may feel guilty. She can memorise verses that confirm her worth in God's eyes, as well as verses that talk about God's goodness, power, and compassion. Isaiah 61 is a powerful passage for rape victims that promises a crown of beauty for ashes and hope of complete restoration through God's healing power.

HIV/AIDS

There are many people in our communities and in our churches who are HIV positive or have AIDS. It is important that as leaders in our churches we have a solid knowledge of the facts about HIV and AIDS so that we are able to respond to the needs people have. We need to offer Jesus' love, compassion and hope to people who are facing the consequences of this disease, regardless of how they contracted it. As we come alongside them, we can counsel them to live positively spiritually, emotionally, and physically.

People will have different needs depending on which stage of the disease they are in. A person who is recently diagnosed HIV positive will likely be going through the different stages of grief. They may need to forgive the person who infected them. They may need to confess their sin of promiscuity or infidelity in order to mend relationships with God and others. A person in a later stage may need help to take her medication regularly or to eat a balanced diet.

Regardless of the stage of their disease, everyone can be encouraged to give their whole life to Jesus and live for Him. This provides a purpose for living and hope for the future.

Conclusion

This summary of counselling principles and situations is just the beginning. We hope you will continue to grow and learn as you walk alongside others on the journey of becoming more like Christ and living for Him.

Questions to think about and discuss:

1 Share about a time when a counsellor or friend helped you through a difficult problem. What things did they do that were most helpful to you?

2. What are some ways that a pastor's wife can help her husband or her local church in the area of counselling?
3. Of all the qualities of a good counsellor described in this chapter, which ones are your strongest? Your weakest?
4. Do you agree that the most important skill a counsellor must have is to listen well? Why or why not?
5. Try this exercise with a friend: Ask your friend to speak for 5 minutes on any topic that interests her. Ask her to include thoughts and feelings about the topic. You as the listener should listen with full attention but without saying anything. Do not interrupt, comment or ask questions. When your friend is finished, talk about how you felt as the listener, and how she felt as the speaker. What was helpful? Was anything uncomfortable?[7]

> They are asking us to leave the manse. Where will we go?

> How do I go back to being an "ordinary" Christian?

Chapter 12

Widowhood and the Ministry

Khumsa Myrtle Mamane

The people who broke the news were not direct. They mentioned an accident—they did not speak of death. It was only twenty-four hours later, when I saw most of our close friends coming to our place, that I grasped the truth—my pastor, friend and husband was dead. The shock was such that I did not cry as one might expect. I remained indifferent for quite some time. Gradually the Lord helped me to face and deal with the reality.

It was end of January and my husband had just told me of his 1990 New Year resolutions including the starting of a primary school for the community, building a house for us, talking to the chief about a church site, having a pre-school, devising a way of being a self-supporting church planter: YHO! How on earth were all these plans going to materialize?

And now, I was a widow at 35 having been comfortably married for eleven years with four children between the ages of nine and four. Life has been a journey. The Lord has been with me.

Emotions

Widows face many challenges in their lives. One of the first is handling their emotions. You will experience many painful emotions as a young widow, and may express them in ways that you regret later. As you mature and heal your emotions will settle. I do cry sometimes, but I usually cry before the Lord, not in front of people. James 5:13 says, "Is any one of you in trouble? He should pray." The Psalms can help you to express your feelings to God. You have been a pastor's wife. You have comforted many people in their grief. Now it is time for God to comfort you.

It is good to control your emotions around your children. You are the only parent for your children now. They depend on you for emotional support. They will lose confidence and trust in you if you are a crying mother all the time. Tell them with words how you are feeling and help them to talk about their feelings, too. I would cry at night when the kids were asleep. If I felt the tears coming on I would go outside to the garden and cry until I had really cried it all out.

In our culture, a new widow does not go anywhere alone. Have a close friend or relative go with you to the bank, post office, or police station. You may have business to conduct in sorting out your husband's affairs. Going to a police station or bank as a new widow can be very trying. I was at the police station looking for a certain form to be filed. They just ignored me. I just felt like screaming and shouting. The next day, I woke up earlier than usual. I arrived at the police station and sat where I had sat the previous day. I kept quiet and did not answer any of their questions. When they realized that I was on a sit-in strike, they prepared the form, put it in an envelope and gave it to me.

Cultural Expectations

There are many cultural expectations for widows. For example in some communities, people expect a widow to dress in a certain way for a year—black, green or blue attire—to show that she is in mourning. To me, mourning is like fasting. It is not necessary to set yourself apart and show everyone you are grieving. Some may say you must eat certain foods or sit or greet in a certain way. As a Christian and a pastor's widow, you may be grieving, but you still have the hope of heaven and confidence in God's sovereign plan. Continuing to dress in the way you always dressed and act as you did when your husband was alive is a way to testify to God's goodness.

In the book of Ruth, Boaz married Ruth to protect and provide for her and her family. In African culture, we have the *ngena* custom—one of your husband's brothers may take you as his wife. This custom has its roots in protecting the widow and her family, but does not serve that purpose any longer. This custom can cause problems for a Christian widow. You must only take a Christian husband if you remarry. It takes courage to stand on Christian principles against the expectations of your husband's family if they are not believers.

For one pastor's wife, when her husband died, the unbelieving family members wanted him to be buried in the garden to watch over the family. But the pastor had made it very clear that when he died he did not want to be buried in the garden, but in a cemetery. So this pastor's wife had to lift up her head in the middle of her grief and insist to the family that his wishes be carried out. The husband's family then refused to contribute anything to the funeral. But God honoured her decision by providing through the generosity of churches, friends, and other pastors.

It is a tough job to live and fight for the biblical culture. The Word of God tells us to conduct ourselves in a manner worthy of the gospel of Christ (Philippians 1:27). Ask God for a character and lifestyle that is pleasing to the Lord.

Relationships

Another challenging adjustment for new widows is in the area of relationships. Starting to go places alone without your friend and husband is uncomfortable. I understand why some widows remain in their shelters to run their own marathons. When I attend a function and I see all the couples standing together and being seated together, I feel like stepping back away from everyone. Sometimes the ushers don't even seem to notice a single woman.

But we widows need relationships with different types of people—in our family, our church, and in the community. We need to ask the Lord to provide us with good friends. Proverbs 17:17 says, "A friend loves at all times, and a brother is born for adversity." Stick to friendship that comes from *agape*—the love of God. Be friends with pastors and their wives. Be friends with other widows, young and old. Organise picnics or house parties with other singles who have children. We were members of a Christian couples' meeting. Some couples dropped off as friends after my husband died. One or two still are my friends, emotional supporters, and advisors.

God provided in a unique way for me in the area of the need for friends. There was a young missionary woman who needed to learn isiXhosa. So she came to live with me on weekends and kept my mind and hands full in the early days after my husband's death. Make friends with younger widows. Give them support in their grief. Their husbands may be with the Lord, but He is a father to the fatherless (Psalm 68:6).

You can befriend Christian men without any strings attached. There are widowers and bachelors who may enjoy your friendship as brothers in Christ. Jesus befriended ladies—Mary and Martha's friendship was facilitated by God's love. But, you must be cautious with your emotions. Paul recommends that a young widow remarry (1 Timothy 5: 11-15). This is a good idea if you can find a godly man who loves the Lord.

There are many temptations to immorality for a new widow. You must always act in an upright way. You may find that married women don't trust you and feel uncomfortable around you. Sometimes it has happened that a married man volunteers to look after the needs in a widow's home—fixing the gate or a cupboard door. This can lead to problems if the wife is not happy with his decision to help you. It is a good idea to have the wife and husband come for a visit together while the husband does some odd jobs around the house. If you can afford it, hire someone to do the work you need done. Also, watch out for men who may not have the best motives, but who volunteer to help for personal or ungodly reasons. You may need to be strong and refuse their help.

You may also receive attractive offers of marriage from rich widowers or single men. You may be tempted to marry for the security, but later find out that his background, commitment to Christ, and extended family are not what is best. If you are to remarry, God will supply the right man in the right time. Be patient and wait for him.

Personal Growth

As a widow you may not feel the need to care for yourself physically as much as you used to. Remember that your body is a temple of God. We can honour God with our body (1 Corinthians 6:19-20). So, be clean, dress well, eat well and get exercise. This can do a lot of good and give you some confidence.

It may happen that your husband was the one who did the banking, fixed leaks, attended workshops and courses. You as a pastor's wife were busy with your responsibilities at home and in church. Now that you are a widow, there are many skills you will need to learn. Stand up and go for that computer course. Enroll with a driving school if you do not have a drivers' licence. Learn how to use your cell phone. Read good books. Be current on issues at the church and in the community. You will need to make decisions alone that you and your husband once made together. God can give you the wisdom you need (James 1:5).

Financial Provision

Paul gives many instructions in I Timothy 5:3-16 concerning widows. A widow's family has the main responsibility to look after her. The church is to look after widows who are really in need. A widow who is over sixty and is known for her godliness can be supported by the church. Younger widows are expected to live godly lives. If they are being tempted to sin, they should marry. So, widows who are healthy and energetic need to work and provide for themselves financially. It is comforting to look back and see how God has provided for me and my children. They were young when my husband died. Now they have all grown up, God provided for them to attend tertiary institutions, and all are living for the Lord. God is good.

Can you believe it? Ordinary gardening can bring a lot of satisfaction, as well as provide meals for growing offspring. My husband was a worker for ACAT, a Christian organization that specializes in agriculture. Just after our marriage we had a lovely garden at a school cottage where we used to work together for two hours in the afternoons. Even after my husband was gone, I still had that passion for gardening. I enjoy looking at the green crops and planning what to plant next. Proverbs 12:11 says that the one who works his land will have abundant food. When we have extra harvest, we can give to others or sell to supplement our cash flow. Now that I am older, I do not spend as much time in my garden. But make no mistake—I am very good at instructing and supervising the one who helps with our gardening programme.

Giving

As a widow you may feel that your limited resources prevent you from giving to the Lord as you used to. Your gifts to the work of the Lord do not have to be in large amounts. Give cheerfully from what you have, and don't be afraid to give sacrificially. Remember the story in Mark 12:41-44. One poor widow put two coins into the offering basin. Jesus commented that the widow's offering was the biggest in the eyes of God. She gave all that she had. So, if you are a widow, go ahead and give generously.

What is good about giving all is that you feel God's blessing there and then. I enjoy giving from my meager resources. Ordinary face soaps can mean a lot to students at a Bible school. Small jars of Vaseline in winter for an orphanage are appreciated. Giving a child an orange or a sweet and watching their face beam with happiness is a great reward. The children in my community know me well. Sometimes they will play around my yard. As evening comes I tell them, "It is time to go home now." "But Ma'am, how can we go home when we haven't eaten yet?" So then I know I must quickly cook a bit of pap and open a tin a fish, and give them each a little bit. The Lord has been wonderful. My four children and I have never gone to bed on empty stomachs. Giving when you see a need, giving when you have something extra makes a merry, contented heart.

Spiritual Needs

It was hard to keep the doors open for services so soon after my husband died. I just wanted to leave. But I also wanted to see souls saved and follow through on my husband's vision for our community. Besides, the church was meeting in our home. I had to be there.

Widows have more time to devote to spiritual things. Anna had been married for seven years, and was a widow the rest of her eighty-four years. When we see her at Jesus' presentation at the Temple, we see a woman who had been in the presence of God twenty-four hours a day, fasting and praying (Luke 2:36-38). We need to pray for ourselves, our kids, our extended families, and all kinds of Christian workers. Pray for the conversion of souls world-wide. You are free to pray right round the clock.

Get involved in the work of the Lord. Grab all opportunities for soul-winning. Have fellowship with other Christians as much as possible. Minister to other widows. Christian widows need to know each other, to encourage those who are weak and pray for each other's woes.

You can choose an area or talent to develop. Were you a school teacher, a gospel singer or an agriculturalist before you married? Develop those gifts for the kingdom. You came to God alone—you were called to him before you met your husband. Now you are free to serve him in your singleness.

I thank the Lord for missionary friends who came into our family life a year or so before my husband's death. They introduced me to a ministry called Child Evangelism Fellowship. This ministry has many facets—teacher trainings, Good News Clubs, 5-Day Holiday Clubs, camps, and rallies—which kept me very busy. God developed in me the passion for evangelizing young children at that time, and it continues until now. I believe that this ministry will keep me busy for His sake until I am called to my final home.

Church Relationship with Pastors' Widows

Churches need to look after their pastors' widows. Not all churches have been successful in this regard. Some church constitutions state that six months after a pastor's death the widow must be evicted from the manse. She must be treated as an ordinary church member. This is why it is wise to begin making plans for a retirement home now. Then, you may enjoy that home together in your retirement, or feel secure knowing that you have a home should your husband pass away unexpectedly. In some churches, the pastor's widow receives a salary until she dies. She is given a special ministry if she desires it, and keeps her status as a ministry leader in the church.

Some measure of hospitality may still be expected from a pastor's widow. The area where you live will determine the style of hospitality that you may offer. Show yourself to be a responsible member of the congregation, being punctual to church meetings and diligent when there is some catering and cleaning to be done.

It is difficult to remain for a long time in the church where your husband was a pastor. You are used to seeing things run a certain way in the church. You may once or twice correct the new person, and find your advice not welcome. So it is wise to suppress your opinions, although it is difficult and sometimes painful. Pray that the Lord will intervene and help the new leaders see for themselves what needs to be done. Try to provide ways for them to go to workshops so they can learn from others. Sometimes they will hear new ideas better from someone else besides the former pastor's widow.

Conclusion

Widowhood is a state of existence. Some type of serious reality has hit you, without any reversible options, but you are still you. Now, at 55, I am amazed at how good life can be. It seems as if each day and month and year is sweeter than the one before. The Lord is teaching me new things every day. I believe in marriage as well as I believe in singlehood. Both of these marital states, when they come from the will of God, bring stability to an individual. If you happen to be a widow, and your husband was a pastor, you are not half a person. You still have full power and full ministries to carry on.

I was close to my children all during their growing up years. Now that they are all settled in families, I am feeling unsettled. It is a new phase for me, and I am looking for new ministries to give my life meaning. I am finding time to write, visit old friends, get further training, and serve God in many ways.

So, I may be alone—but I am not LONELY.

Questions to think about and discuss:

1. Have you ever known a pastor's widow? What was she like?
2. What are some of the challenges pastors' widows face?
3. What is God's view of widows (Exodus 22:22-24; Psalm 68:5; Deuteronomy 10:18)?
4. How could the church help widows cope with changes in their lives?
5. What are some ways widows could provide for the needs of their families?
6. How long after losing her husband do you think a pastors' widow should stay at that local church?
7. Find a time to sit down with your pastor husband and discuss your future should he pass away unexpectedly. If you have not already done so, make a simple will using the form provided in Appendix 2.

Resources for widows:

J. O. Sanders, *Facing Loneliness*, (Grand Rapids, Michigan: Discovery House Publishers, 1988)

Jan Sheble, *Hope and Help for the Widow*, (Chattanooga, Tennessee: AMG Publishers, 2003)

> There are always more needs to meet. When am I supposed to rest?

> Visiting orphans after work, cooking for the family, Bible study, UNISA course...I am SO TIRED!

> We know Sunday is not a day of rest for the pastor and his family!

Chapter 13

Rest and Refreshment in Ministry

Susan Binion

Sometimes it seems that when we get to heaven, we hope to hear Jesus say, "Well done, thou tired and busy servant!" We may even wear our tiredness and busyness as a badge of spirituality and think that being too busy is what is expected of pastors' wives.

If you were to choose one word that would summarise Jesus' life on earth, what would it be? You might think of *holy*, or *obedient*, or *purposeful*, or even *busy*. One mature Christian leader suggested this word: *relaxed*. Are you surprised by his suggestion? Think of Jesus asleep in the boat in the middle of a storm, or calmly feeding 5000 people. Think of his remarks to Martha, who was worried and bothered about so many things. Jesus always seemed to be at peace—*relaxed*—in the midst of a busy schedule and the compelling needs that surrounded him.

At different seasons of my life, I have found myself becoming very busy with ministry and family, neglecting my time with God each morning. I would become very dry spiritually, and sometimes on the verge of breaking down emotionally. Each time, God, who loves me and knows my deepest needs, intervened to rescue me.

Finally, ten years ago, I broke my hip and had to be on crutches for five months. During that time, I couldn't even get myself a glass of water. I felt useless to my family and to God. I also had to take a certain medicine before breakfast every morning. Afterwards, I had to sit quietly for thirty minutes before I could eat breakfast. It occurred to me that I could use that time for reading my Bible and praying. I see that time as a gentle rebuke from the Lord that forced me back into the habit of spending time with him at the beginning of each day. Since that experience, I have learned many things about staying close to God and being refreshed in ministry.

Finding Rest

Jesus said, "Come to me, all you who are weary and burdened, and I will give you rest. Take my yoke upon you and learn from me, for I am gentle and humble in heart, and you will find rest for your souls. For my yoke is easy and my burden is light" (Matthew 11:28-30).

In ministry, you may come to the place where you are "soul-weary". You do not seem to have another piece of yourself to offer to anyone, and you may not even care. Yet our Master offers rest so freely and lovingly. It is interesting to me that in this verse Jesus doesn't offer to take our yoke away from us, just to replace it with his.

In the past, when I read this verse, I used to picture Jesus putting a yoke on my shoulders which was connected to a cart carrying a burden. One day, a Xhosa pastor explained to me about yokes and oxen. He said that a young, untrained ox will not willingly allow himself to be yoked to a plow or cart. But, if you put an older, experienced ox on one side of the yoke, the younger ox will just walk right up and put his head into the other side. So now when I read this verse, I picture Jesus on one side of the yoke, pulling with me, teaching me how to serve him.

One way to truly find rest is to understand and practice the principle of a sabbath rest. As Lynne Baab explains in her book, *Sabbath Keeping*[1], this does not mean to observe the Jewish Sabbath and all of its laws on Saturdays. Nor does it mean to create a Christian Sabbath on Sundays and follow certain rules about what one may or may not do.

The *principle* of a sabbath rest is found in Scripture from the very beginning of Genesis. God made the whole world and everything in it, and then rested on the seventh day. The word "rested" in Genesis 2:1 and 2 in Hebrew is s*habath*, which means to "cease" or "stop". By resting on the seventh day, God blessed it and set it apart from the other six days. This is even before the Ten Commandments were given in Exodus 20, where God is proclaims a day of *rest from customary work*—for men, women, children, servants and animals.

In Deuteronomy 5:12 to 15, God repeats the Sabbath commandment, but gives another reason for it. Here he reminds the Israelites that when they were slaves in Egypt, they were forced to work seven days a week. But now they are *free* to work for six days and then rest on the seventh.

In Leviticus 23:3 the Sabbath is called a day of rest and *sacred assembly*, so it is also a time of worship, meeting with others, and learning about God.

In Exodus 16 we read the story of God's *provision* for the Israelites by giving them manna to eat. He made it clear that by not collecting manna on the Sabbath, they were expressing their trust in God. They knew he would provide extra the day before so that they would have enough to eat on the Sabbath. Observing the Sabbath by not buying and selling (Nehemiah 10:31; 13:15-22) also showed the people's satisfaction and *contentment* with what God had already provided.

So in the Old Testament the Sabbath meant rest from customary work, an expression of freedom, a time for sacred assembly, a demonstration of trust in God's provision, and contentment with what he had given.

In the New Testament Jesus proclaims that he is Lord of the Sabbath. He demonstrated that the Sabbath was intended for people's good by setting people free from illness, blindness and the bondage of Satan on this holy day. The Sabbath was to be seen as a blessing, not a burden.

Benefits of a Sabbath Rest

While Acts 15 and other New Testament passages make it clear that non-Jewish Christians are not bound to any Sabbath laws, the principle of a sabbath rest is built into the way the world works from creation. There are great benefits to taking a regular time off each week from our customary work.

The principle of rest teaches us *grace*. Taking time off from our regular work and ministry testifies to our understanding that we cannot earn God's love or his blessing by what we do. It may show us that our self-esteem has been bound up in our accomplishments, not our relationship with God through Jesus Christ.

By allowing ourselves to rest on a regular basis, we are expressing our understanding that *the work is God's, not ours.* If God could make the world in six days, our "to-do" list can't be longer than that! There must be a time in each week where we can say, "I have done what you have asked me to do," and rest from our work.

Observing a day of rest demonstrates our *trust in God's provision* and develops in us a grateful spirit for what we already have. It is a statement of faith against the world system which cries, "Produce! Possess! Accomplish!" A spirit of contentment and thankfulness is great gain, according to I Timothy 6:6. Resting from work says, "I have enough time, enough goods, enough self-esteem." We also gain freedom from things that may otherwise enslave us or are becoming idols in our lives.

Many people who regularly observe a day of rest in their lives also testify that they have more energy the rest of the week to press ahead with the demanding tasks that face them.

Getting Practical

It is not easy for people in ministry to find time to rest. In some areas, church members believe that the pastor must always be available, twenty-four/seven, or he is not a good pastor. If you believe that God is calling you to rest on a regular basis, ask him to show you and your husband how to educate the congregation in this area. If you live on the mission property, you may have to find another place to go for the day, to avoid interruptions.

Everyone needs a day of rest, not just the pastor's family. As a congregation, you could choose a day not to interrupt one another with phone calls or visits. One group of Christians decided together that Monday afternoons would be their day of rest. Those that were employed returned straight home in the afternoon. No one went to town to shop or conduct business. They ended the day with community prayer at 5 pm. To keep Sundays more restful, those with refrigerators could cook ahead on Saturdays, leaving Sundays free for fellowship and worship.

What kinds of things do you think God wants you to rest from? Besides ministry or regular work obligations, are you studying for a course? Do you need to rest from the computer or cell phone or television? Do you need to cease shopping and be content with what you have? What about resting from anxiety or grudges? If you ask the Lord, he will show you how to make your day a restful expression of your dependence on him.

What kinds of activities would you like to include on your day of rest? Again, ask the Lord to guide you. For people in ministry, going to a service may not be restful. Setting aside a special time for private worship, giving God all of your heart and attention like Mary did, may be more what is needed. You may want to make this a day of family togetherness, or a time to pursue a creative hobby. Spending time in God's creation, getting exercise, or even playing a sport can be a restful activity. One pastor used to spend every Monday in his vegetable and flower gardens. The combination of exercise, being in the outdoors, and creating beauty was a refreshing day well-spent. He also had time to reflect on the week and talk to God as he worked with his hands.

Refreshment

Keeping up with daily demands of family, ministry and work can drain our spiritual resources as ministry wives. Communication with our heavenly Father will keep us connected to the life-giving vine of God's power and peace. Jesus often went off on his own to pray, sometimes spending all night in prayer. We can do the same by making time each day to pray and study God's word. We have seen that a weekly time of rest from our work has many benefits for us spiritually, emotionally, and physically. Many Christians, especially those in ministry, have also found that a quarterly or yearly retreat helps them to stay refreshed in the Lord. This doesn't mean attending a conference with many other people and spending time in meetings all day. A yearly retreat could be a day, a weekend, or even a week that you spend alone with God, reading his word, fasting, praying, and asking him to show you his path for your year ahead.

You and your husband could spend part of the time individually with the Lord, and then come together to share the insights you have gained. You would need to make arrangements to stay in a place where you will not be interrupted by the telephone, or by the needs of the church or work. Many who have done this testify that God often gives them fresh direction and power for ministry during these times of retreat, as well as renewing their marriage relationship.

Another way to stay refreshed in the Lord is to meet regularly with others in ministry, especially with other pastors' wives. There is no one who understands your challenges and heartaches like another ministry wife. Seek out other pastors' wives to meet with regularly—not to plan ladies' teas or denominational conferences—but to cry on each others' shoulders, to pray for each other and your families, and to rejoice in the special blessings that God brings to those in ministry. Don't be afraid to look beyond denominational boundaries to find women who share your circumstances and your heart for ministry.

Knowing God's priorities for your life and living according to them is another way to reduce stress and live a refreshed life. At a retreat for pastors' wives, one young wife said, "I'm doing too much at church—always filling the gaps that others leave. People expect me to do this because I'm the pastor's wife." Knowing how God has gifted you, and putting most of your time into ministry that uses those gifts, will save you from overloading your day with everyone else's plans for your life. If you are beginning in a church planting ministry, you may find yourself wearing many hats at first, and serving in many areas where you feel unqualified. But remember that the primary goal of pastoral ministry is to equip *others* for service, so that *they* can build up the body of Christ (Ephesians 4:12). Your aim should be to train people and delegate to them, not to rob them of opportunities to develop their gifts and grow to maturity. Being able to say "no" to some ministry opportunities gives you a chance to rest and another person a chance to grow.

Conclusion

My husband and I were talking one day with a more experienced pastor's wife about being overloaded in ministry. As is often the case in ministry marriages, he was defending a very busy schedule, and I was trying to convince him we needed more time for each other and the family. He finally said, "I would rather *burn out* than *rust out*." The pastor's wife replied, "Well, there *are* other options."

Certainly, we do not want to "rust out" in ministry. We always want to be examples of diligence in every area of our lives. We know that the ministry is a calling to a life of sacrifice, not just an eight-to-five job. But do we want to burn out like the fireworks at Soccer City during the World Cup, shining brilliantly for a few years of ministry and then having nothing left to give? There is another option. We can stay connected to the Vine of Jesus Christ through regular times of rest and refreshment. Jesus is looking for "good and faithful" servants, not "tired and busy" ones. By taking time to rest, we show God that we delight in him above all.

Questions to think about and discuss:[2]

1. What do you remember about "sabbath" practices in your family or community growing up?

2. If God were to ask you to stop doing something for twenty-four hours a week, what might it be?

3. What fears do you have and what obstacles do you expect in trying to keep a day of rest?

4. If you were going to take twenty-four hours off from "customary work", what would you need to do ahead of time to prepare?

5. What activities would you like to do on your day of rest?

6. Do you have daily times with God in prayer and his word? What are some of the blessings you have found with this habit? If not, what do you need to change to make it happen?

7. What would be the benefits for your marriage and ministry if you took a yearly spiritual retreat?

Chapter 14

Conclusion: The Ministry Received

Clare Zasembo Mambi

A pastor's wife—what a name! If you had married a plumber, you would not be known as a plumber's wife. The wife of a teacher does not receive the special title of "Teacher's Wife." Only the wife of a man called to do God's work is called "pastor's wife" or "ministry wife." As we have journeyed through these chapters much has been shared. We have seen that we can make it together with God. God has so much in store for us.

A story is told of a man who was travelling from Durban to London by ship. He bought himself a few packets of biscuits for his provision, since it was going to take two weeks to travel to London. When it was time for everyone to have dinner, he remained in his cabin to munch on his biscuits. This continued for days and it was beginning to tell. He lost weight and was becoming weaker. When asked why he did not join the rest of the passengers in the dining hall, he said he could not afford the expensive food that was served there. Poor man—he did not realise that the sea fare included all the meals! This happens to us as God's children. We either forget about, or we are unaware of, the riches which are available to us as His chosen ones.

Sometimes this attitude of not taking risks or trusting God's promises could be due to a fear of failure. This can paralyse us. God has not given us a spirit of fear, but of power and love (2 Timothy 1:7). Therefore, if we fear, we know it is not God's doing, but our own. We have an abundance of riches in Christ. In 1 Peter 1:4 we are told that we have been called "to obtain an inheritance which is imperishable and undefiled and will not fade away, reserved in heaven for you." (NASB) If such is the greatness of our inheritance, it is worth fighting for. In addition to our inheritance, we can know the surpassing greatness of His power. How great is that power? It is like the working of His mighty strength which He brought about in Christ (Ephesians 1:19-20). This resurrection power is available to us to do every good work and win every battle we encounter.

Ministry wife, fight the good fight of the faith (1 Timothy 6:12). It was this fight that Paul was talking about when he declared, even as he faced death, "I have fought the good fight, I have finished the race, I have kept the faith" (2 Timothy 4:7-8). God has promised so many rewards, both now and in eternity, to those who endure at all times, under all circumstances, giving glory to God. The joy of knowing that we are in His will, doing His work gives satisfaction to our souls. The apostle John in Revelation 2 tells us of the future blessings promised to the faithful: we will eat of the tree of life, we will receive a crown of life, we will not be hurt by the second death, and we will be given authority over the nations.

In Revelation 3 the promises continue for those who overcome:

- They will walk with Christ.
- Their names will not be erased from the book of life.
- Christ will confess them before God and His angels.
- They will be kept from the hour of testing.
- They will be made pillars in God's temple.
- Christ will write the name of God and the city of God upon them.
- They will be granted to sit with Christ on His throne as He also overcame and sat with the Father on His throne.

If these blessings were to be called "earnings," everyone would boast about their achievement. But they are all by God's grace.

Working with people is a privilege from God. You learn to love them, and they also love you. If you are comfortable with yourself, others will be comfortable with you. As you minister to other ladies you will meet different types of people whose lives will encourage you. I once met a lady who should have been a very depressed person. Everything about her life since childhood was not right. She married a believer, but then her husband backslid. The children did not finish school and misbehaved. She is the sole breadwinner in the family. The in-laws blame her for everything. She has every reason to be bitter. But listen to what she says: "Sometimes I laugh, sometimes I cry. But God and I will make it." And I believe she will make it. She uses the experiences of her life to minister to those with similar hurts. She is a blessing, and you are sure to learn one or two things from her as you spend time with her. As God entrusts you with people who come to you with different needs and sensitive issues, remember that you must be confidential. Try not to carry other people's problems yourself—give them to God.

In testing times some become angry and think that God does not love them. In such times you should emulate Leah who brought her sorrows to God. She knew God heard her cry. Although she was not beautiful like Rachel, she had peace in her heart as she was convinced that God loved her as a valuable person. She stopped complaining about difficulties and said, "This time I will praise the Lord." This is attested to by the name she gave her fourth son Judah, which means "praise" (Genesis 29:35). Judah, the son of unloved Leah, is Jesus' ancestor (Matthew 1:2, 3, 16). You, as a ministry wife, need to display a godly character when times are difficult. God is there to help you and to accomplish the work He has started in you.

For some women, the testing does not come in difficult times, but in times of abundance and opportunity. These days the focus in the South African context is on empowering women. The government and other companies offer qualified women highly paid positions with much prestige and the opportunity for travel and for further study. While it is good to empower women, sometimes this economic empowerment comes at the expense of women's families and spiritual life. As a pastor's wife, you may be qualified for such positions, and it is possible that you can balance all of God's priorities for your marriage, family, spiritual life and ministry along with this kind of employment. But as a Christian woman, remember that your ultimate goal is to please your Master and Saviour in everything. Only what you invest in *His* kingdom will last forever. He will reward you. If you find that your employer's goals conflict with God's priorities, you may need to think carefully about your choice of employment.

When a group of government employees were orientated for their job they were told they were public servants—all they would be doing would be in public. One of them always drank a lot after work. When confronted he said, "I have the right to do what I like when I am off duty." He was told that he was a public servant twenty four hours a day, seven days a week. We are also Christ's slaves. When we have done everything our Master asks us to do, we cannot boast, but rather say, "We have only done our duty" (Luke 17:7-10). The slave has no rights, no will of his own. He has to choose his master's will. This is the attitude we need to have. We need to know that we are fully accountable to our Master.

Young ministry wife, know that without your participation the work of God will not be as effective as it should be. This is your chance to shine for the Lord. Do as He wills. Do the work diligently. With our prayers and love we support you. We understand what you are experiencing—some of these situations we also have gone through. But God helped us, and He will see you through.

Sarah is an example of gentleness, obedience and respect for her husband in spite of the many difficulties she encountered in her married life with Abraham. She was willing to travel with her husband wherever he went. She obeyed her husband and called him "lord". Even in her very old age she was still willing to sleep with her husband! It may happen that you face what Sarah faced. Learn to wait upon God. He knows what is best for you. Be who you are and don't try to imitate others. There is only one you. No one can do what are placed here on earth to do. Just excel in being who you are. As you consistently do these things you will develop fitness–the type of fitness that will make you useful to the Master, prepared for every good work. You will benefit others with your ministry. You will bear much fruit, both in your own character and in bringing others to the Lord.

In Colossians 4:17 Paul tells one leader in the young church to "take heed to the ministry which you have received in the Lord, that you may fulfill it" (NKJV). As a pastor's wife, you have received a ministry from the Lord: to support your husband by serving the Lord Jesus in the unique way he has designed you to do. May you experience God's richest blessings as you fulfil the ministry He has given to you.

Postscript

A Word from a Young Pastor's Wife

At a retreat for ministry wives Mandisa Khomo, a young pastor's wife, shared the following encouragement and advice:

There was a time in my life when I had no joy or peace. I thought it was because of the circumstances I was facing and the people around me.

I remember I had a supervisor who was very difficult to work with. In my mind I thought she was a bad person and I was a good person. We used to argue at work even to the point of getting warnings. I thought the reason I was not happy at work was because of her. In reality, the reason I was unhappy was because I had lost my joy and I didn't know what it meant to walk in the love of God. I did not have the character of Christ.

I was at war outwardly because there was a *war going on inwardly*. During this time I thought I was a perfect Christian, but I lived a yoyo Christian life—some days I was down, some days up. The reality was I could not connect well with God. It was difficult for me to pray because my heart was so cluttered. I had excuses for my condition, and guess what? People with excuses never change in life and never grow spiritually. I was that type of a Christian who knew the Word, went to church, and paid my tithes—but I did not apply the Word in my life. I used it to judge, criticize and see every wrong thing in other people. I forgot to judge myself because I was deceived by the devil into thinking that I was perfect.

I came to a point in life where I stopped trying to change others, and I said, "God change me." When I prayed that prayer God began to show me my weaknesses, and I gradually changed. I began to take the Word seriously. One morning as I was praying these words came into my heart: *"Reading the Word of God is about transformation, not compliance."* Most of us read the Word to comply outwardly with what a good Christian looks like. We are told to read the Word every day and to share with others. Now my daily exercise is to read the Word in order to be transformed. Doing this has changed my life. I have more joy, peace, patience, and love. I am able to see people through God's eyes and I have compassion for them.

From this experience, I have learned that character building is very important. Your character is what determines how long you will stand or how far you will go in your Christian walk. You may have an anointing or a call or a gift, but if you don't allow God to build your character, you will fall. The devil will use the things in your character that do not please God to pull you down. The anointing comes freely; character must be worked on.

Every fall or defeat in a Christian's life can be traced back to an area of disobedience which has been ignored for a long time. The bells do ring, the Holy Spirit speaks, but we ignore His voice. We ignore what the Bible says about a certain area of our life, we do not listen when a sister or brother in the Lord corrects us, but instead follow our mind, our flesh or our desires.

We can end up living a yo-yo Christian life because we do not have the character of Christ in us. We talk as the world talks, we live as the world lives and we do the things that non-Christians do. We forget that we belong to God, and we are called to resemble Him.

The question you can ask yourself today is, "Who do I resemble?"

If you want to progress in life or go far with God, you must allow God to build your character. The impurities that you allow in your life hinder God from blessing you and your ministry. You may even think that God has forsaken you or does not love you. But God is waiting for you to be willing to change. Then His Holy Spirit can go to work.

I was praying a prayer that said, "Lord, change *them!*" But God was more interested in changing me first. We will only be used to the fullest by God as pastors' wives when we allow God to build our character and grow the fruit of the Spirit—love, joy, peace, patience, kindness, goodness, faithfulness, gentleness and self-control (Galatians 5:22-25).

Do you know what happened after I began to ask God to change me? God began to change the people around me. I learned that people are not as interested in what I have to say as they are interested in my conduct. They are not changed by my words, but won by my actions. Although we try very hard to change others, only God has power to change another human being. Hand over the person to God and do what is right—obey the Word—and you will see people changing. By allowing God to change my character, my supervisor also changed and we had peace at work. Going to work was no longer a burden, but joy to me. Ever since then I have been growing spiritually, I have a more peaceful life, and God uses me to help other people.

I made this resolution after this great change in my life: *no matter how I feel, God's way will always win in my life because I have discovered that His way is perfect. My ways always fail me.*

Appendix 1

Surviving Bible School

Khumsa Mamane and Susan Binion

If your husband received a call to the ministry after you were married, it is likely that at some point he will want to pursue further training at a seminary or Bible college. This will begin a new adventure for you, his wife, as your faith is refined in new ways, and your love for your husband is put to the test. Some couples must live apart during their husband's years of study. Some wives are fortunate to accompany their husbands, and they may even study themselves. Some may follow their husbands, but be forced to leave children behind with relatives. In any case, there may be some people who do not understand your decision. You may even doubt it yourselves from time to time. Perhaps you have heard some comments like these below:

> "Just think of it! Brother Kunene has resigned his job as a policeman to go to Bible college. How will his boys register for high school? I can't understand why some folks must run away from their family responsibilities, making God's work a scapegoat."

> "I so wish that my husband may be well-trained at a Bible school. I am certain that the Lord will provide for our basic needs even if he leaves his business for three years. The Word of God says many good things about those who follow Jesus all the way. Matthew 19:27 says, 'We have left everything to follow you....' Surely there will be blessing along with our sacrifice?"

> "Some brethren can be crazy. Did you hear that both Mamanes have resigned their teaching posts to go to Seminary? It was first the man and now the wife. We are busy here buying houses on our government subsidy. Will they ever have a house of their own? What about the education of their children?"

"There is absolutely no need for Christians to go to a Bible school. If you are gifted, you can preach and perform the miracles that Jesus did. My husband and I can lead our local church, yet we have not gone to any Bible school. And look, the church is growing like any other church."

"I am so happy that we were convinced the Lord was leading us to attend Bible school. We learnt a lot about God's presence whenever we had to make decisions. Psalm 57:2 says, "I'll cry to God who performs all things for me." So it has been for us. Goodness and mercy have always followed us."

We meet regularly with the wives of the students at Union Bible Institute who are able to come to campus. We once asked them about their greatest struggles as wives of students. Here is a summary of what they said:

One of the hardest things for many was the *change of lifestyle* that they had to undergo as a family. It was especially difficult to watch their children make adjustments. Some were used to being dropped off at school, and now they had to learn to ride taxis. Perhaps they even had to change schools. They could no longer afford as many new clothes.

Often there were *financial pressures* and bills to pay. The pressure of providing for the family now fell on the wife's shoulders, and it could feel very heavy. If she was distracted or worried, she might not perform as well at work.

There was the problem of *loneliness*, and of having to be both father and mother—sometimes to difficult teenagers. Younger children could not understand why their father was gone. Living apart put much stress on the marriage. Often, crises came in the middle of exam week or when a paper was due, and the wife did not want to burden her husband with concerns from home. So she had to bear it alone.

If the wife followed the husband to Bible college, but the *children* had to stay at home, there was the added concern for their well-being and the guilt that sometimes came with separation.

We also asked the women about what blessings they had experienced as wives of Bible college students. They were enthusiastic in their answers. Most of them had experienced *God's provision* in miraculous ways. One woman shared how she had sought a teaching job for ten years. At first, she was not in favour of her husband's decision to study. But when she finally released him, God opened the door to the teaching job she had always wanted.

Most of the women admitted that they had depended on their husbands' faith in times of crisis. Now that their husbands were away, they were forced to *rely on God for themselves*, and their faith grew as a result.

One pastors' wife shared that when her husband was studying overseas, their eldest son became very ill at boarding school. She received a call from the hospital asking her to come and sign the consent form for her son's surgery. She had to rush to the hospital, and there was no time to phone her husband. The Lord was good—the surgery was successful.

Another time, her daughter was waiting for acceptance to university. The day came for the university to open, and they had not yet received a letter of acceptance. On faith, she drove to the university. All of the other prospective students were asked to leave their cars outside. She drove up to the gate, and the guard opened for her without asking any questions. The university allowed her daughter to register. Later that week, they finally received the letter—stating that her daughter had *not* been accepted! Yet she was already beginning her studies. Once again, the Lord had provided.

We asked the wives of UBI students to share with us the verses of Scripture that helped them the most while their husbands were studying. These verses can serve as weapons against the enemies of doubt and fear that can steal your joy and peace as you face life as the wife of a Bible college student. Take time to look up each one and apply it to your own situation. Write them out and put them where you can see them often. And be encouraged that God is true to His Word, ready to meet your needs. They are shown opposite here.

What follows is a testimony from one of our authors, Khumsa Mamane, with words of encouragement for any woman whose husband is thinking about studying full-time for ministry.

> My conversion during my teenage years was an exciting adventure for me. The mention of the name of Jesus still brings joy and hope to me. As I was growing up in the Lord I had a burning desire to be part of the team that works in the

> Proverbs 3:5-6
> Matthew 6:33-34
> Philippians 2:12-13
> Luke 1:37, 46-47
> Psalm 34:18
> Psalm 121:1
> Isaiah 40

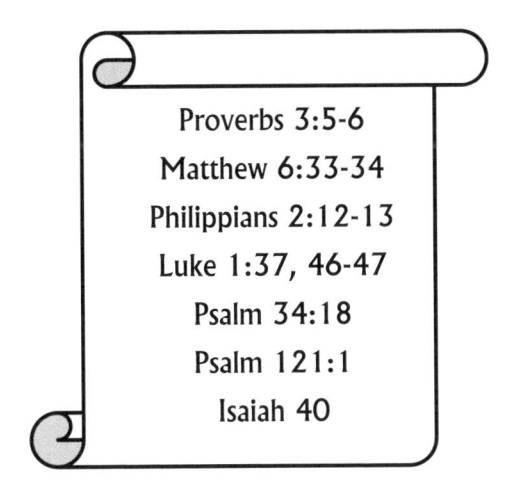

vineyard of the Lord. I am also grateful that after accepting Jesus as Lord and Saviour, I had some mentors who gave me good reasons to start each day of my life with quiet time in God's Word and prayer. My passion for reading the Word of God, Christian books and magazines planted in me the desire to learn more about the mighty works of God. Maybe, I thought, Bible school attendance would be the best thing for me to do. Guess what? The Lord gave me marriage first instead of Bible school. I got married to an "ordinary" Christian. He had skill in preaching and evangelizing, but was not Bible school educated.

Our prayers for attending Bible school came at an unexpected time for our young family. After attending our church's December conference where the speaker strongly challenged everyone to study the Word of God, my husband quit his job and enrolled in seminary to start January of the following year.

We did not have much time to think about sponsors and support. At the seminary the principal and Council helped him to get a sponsor for tuition and books. Food and transport were still lacking. And I was left behind at my hometown—it was very painful to be apart.

My husband wanted me to be with him—we wanted to be together. So in the second year, I joined him. I was not anxious about quitting my job—I just put in my letter of resignation and off we went. It wasn't a heavy decision. My husband had already taken the decision, and I was following my leader with something that I also wanted to do. He was confident. You look down the corridor and you don't know what is there, but you trust things will be well by faith.

So I left home to join my student husband as a student wife, with two kids and one on the way. There was no provision at the seminary for such people at that time. The sponsors that were there made it clear that they did not sponsor students' wives and children. Philippians 4:19 "And my God will meet all your needs according to His glorious riches in Christ Jesus" became very real for us.

We had to look for accommodation apart from the other students because we had children—the Lord provided. He also took care of other expenses. Collecting empty 1 litre soft drink bottles became my hobby. These could be exchanged for cash at the grocery store. The cash provided a nice Sunday lunch with meat and salads. There were some Bible school students from Sweetwaters who were helping with Sunday School every week. We always looked forward to their Sunday visit, and we delighted in catering for them as well. Those were the good old days, I tell you. God has and will always provide for needs on a daily basis.

There was a lecturer's wife who had a soft spot for us wives. We met once a week for a Bible lesson. We put memory verses on cards and practiced while we were doing chores. Skills such as baking simple recipes and how to survive on a small budget were shared.

In the Lord's Prayer in Luke 11:3 Jesus taught us to ask for bread on a daily basis. One day, I had cleaned the fridge. There was a jug of water and one tomato in it. The children were playing happily, waiting for the next meal. I was praying hopefully and trusting the Lord for the next meal for us all. A kombi full of our Christian friends from home pulled up on the lawn. We exchanged greetings and hugs. They were on their way to a conference and had decided to spend the night with us. After half an hour, the leader of the group asked for a cold drink, and he just went to the fridge and opened it. To his amazement, he found only the tomato and the water.

He called my husband, "Ntanga, where is your food?" "It is still at the grocery store—go and fetch it," answered my husband. Four members of the group and my husband went to the store and came back with supplies that lasted us for a month. Wonderful! The Lord kept on doing great things for the years whilst my spouse was at the seminary.

God provided all of our needs in amazing ways. The wife of the principal was almost my size. She would now and again call me to their place, open up her wardrobe and ask me to choose any outfit that I liked. Our children didn't always have brand new clothes, but they had enough. Most of their toys were home-made: cars made of wire and balls made of plastic. We have warm memories of those days.

Living one day at a time taught us that God is very much interested in our lives on a daily basis. Looking ahead at the corridors of coming years gives back worry, anxiety, fear and hopelessness. Our Heavenly Father has not called us to that. He has called us to praise His name. Psalm 113:3 says, "From the rising of the sun, till the going down of the same, the Lord's name is to be praised."

The Lord has been our special physician all the way. The kids did not have any serious ailments during the Bible school years. My husband was also healthy and fit, and so was I. We would pray all colds and flus away. My eyes had a problem and I was wearing spectacles. One day, the glasses broke—they fell on a stone and were completely crushed into pieces. There was no hope that we could ever have cash to buy new glasses. So we decided to pray for the total healing of my eyes. My eye problem was solved by the Lord himself. I did not need spectacles after that.

After some time I applied for a job at a school which was eight kilometres from where we stayed. I got the job, praise God. In those days, it usually took two or three months for the government to pay a new employee a salary. Those three months were difficult. We had to have somebody to look after the kids. We had to have bus fare to and from work. On some days, I walked. I praise God because I was healthy enough to do that.

We needed some recreation to keep sound in mind and body. Because of the studies and assignments at the seminary, my husband had little time for recreation. I enjoyed reading and writing even at that time. I would translate tracts into our mother tongue from the English language when original authors wished. Also, editing my husband's assignments was a fun way for me to learn.

Most of our free time we would spend with the children: playing games, memorising Scripture, and singing together. One missionary friend gave us a keyboard for the children. My husband had a guitar and I would be vocalist. The days were difficult, but what we remember are the warm feelings about our time at Bible school.

From the way God has worked in my own life, I can say: If you feel the Master's call, do not fear. He leads you. The Lord always leads us to the right path, just as he led the Israelites by a pillar of fire and a pillar of cloud. You may be married. You may not be married yet. If you feel you must study the Word, go ahead.

If you feel your husband wants to go to Bible school, pray and release him. This is not about economic satisfaction, but spiritual fulfillment. Do not be afraid to quit your job and follow your husband. When the Master has called you, you will not be happy if you don't respond to the call, no matter what job or other commitments you may have.

The Lord doesn't call you and then leave you alone. He'll always be there for you. If you have children, dedicate them to Him. He'll provide for their education and their future.

God specializes in things people think are impossible. He can do what no one else can do.

Appendix 2

Writing a Will[1]

We do not like to think about our own death, or the death of our spouse, but it is a fact that no one can predict the length of his or her life. Preparing a will is an act of love toward those who will remain behind, especially those for whom you have been financially responsible. It prevents misunderstandings between family members, even if you do not feel you have many possessions.

For a will to be a legal document, you must include certain information:

1. The date on which the document has been drawn up and signed.
2. Personal details including all possible addresses of the one making the will.
3. Marital status and type of marriage (in community of property or out of community of property).
4. Names, sex and dates of birth for children.
5. Clarification whether this is a new will or a replacement of a previous will.
6. The name of a person who will take care of the will after your death. Perhaps this will be a trusted friend or another pastor in your denomination.
7. Mention the person or persons to whom you would like to give your Estate/belongings, and include their addresses.
8. Mention any special items and to whom they should be given. This may include livestock in a rural area, or even a wedding ring or special item of clothing.
9. Put your full signature *on every page* of the will.
10. Get two witnesses to sign your will *on every page* as well. They do not have to read the will—just sign that they have seen *you* sign it.

In addition to the above, you should clarify who will look after your children in case both you and your spouse die at the same time. You can specify some things to be kept in trust until the children reach a certain age. Letting your children know that you have a plan for their care can be a great comfort to them.

Sample will:

MY WILL

(What I want to happen to my things and /or my children when I die)

I, (Name and Surname)_____say that this is my last will.

ID Number or date of birth_____

Address_____

Married or single:_____

If married, name of spouse:_____

Names, sex and dates of birth of all children _____

_____

1. This is my last will, and it replaces any other will I might have made before.

2. I would like _____(name of person) to be Executor (take care of my will and see to it that everything happens the way I have asked it to).

3. I would like these special things (clothing, jewellery, house, furniture, etc,) to go to these people:

My (item)_____to (name of person)_____

who lives at this address:_____

My (item)_____to (name of person)_____

who lives at this address:_____

My (item)_____to (name of person)_____

who lives at this address:_____

4. I would like everything else I own to go to _____(name).

5. I would like (name of person) _____to look after my children. (If the children go to different people, name clearly which children should go to which people).

Name of child_____Name of guardian_____

Name of child_____Name of guardian_____

6. I want to make sure that these things are kept in trust for my children for when they are _____years old.

My (item)_____to (name of child)_____

who lives at this address:_____

My (item)_____to (name of child)_____

who lives at this address:_____

My Signature (or thumbprint)_____

Date_____

Signature Witness 1:_____Date:_____

Signature Witness 1:_____ ___Date:_____

About the Authors

Susan Binion has served alongside her husband in South Africa since 1988, first in church planting in the Eastern Cape, and then at the Union Bible Institute in KwaZulu-Natal. She is currently the chairperson of *Sisebenza Kanyekanye*, the ministry to the wives of students at Union Bible Institute. She has four children. Through her interaction with student wives, alumni, and other pastors' wives, God gave her a burden to develop a book that could be used to encourage and prepare women for their unique and influential role as ministry wives.

Khumsa Myrtle Mamane has been serving the Lord for 33 years, first alongside her husband in church planting in the Eastern Cape, and then in children's ministry and literature translation. She trained as a Junior Secondary Teacher and taught for 32 years at various levels, eventually founding and heading a primary school in her own community. She has four grown children. Mrs. Mamane welcomed the opportunity to share her experiences in this book. She hopes that those who read it will feel as if they are on the sofa in her lounge, chatting about the challenges they face as ministry wives, knowing they are supported and loved by others who have travelled the road before them.

Clare Zasembo Mambi has been a pastor's wife for the last 22 years. She has been involved in church planting, hospital and prison ministry, as well as ministry to street children in the Pietermaritzburg area. Before marriage, she was a tent evangelist. She is a graduate of All Africa School of Theology, Applebosch Teacher Training College, and the Evangelical Seminary of Southern Africa. She has five children. She became interested in this project because she wanted a platform to encourage young pastors' wives facing the blessings, joys, and challenges of ministry.

Fikile Octavia Mpunzana began her life in ministry as a pastor's wife immediately after graduating from the Union Bible Institute in 1993. She has served her church primarily in women's ministry, as well as youth and children's work, and is currently pastoring a church in KwaZulu-Natal. She has four children. The opportunity to contribute to this book has inspired and encouraged her. She hopes that this book will open the minds of other pastors' wives and give them wisdom in handling challenges in their families, churches, and communities.

Sonene M. Nyawo has been a pastor's wife for 21 years. She serves her church as coordinator of the praise and worship team and is involved in leadership roles in various women's ministries. She also serves in a couples' ministry with her husband. She has three children. She is a graduate of the University of Swaziland and the University of KwaZulu-Natal. She has been a teacher for the last 22 years, currently lecturing in the department of theology and religious studies at the University of Swaziland. Mrs. Nyawo cherished the time she spent writing for this book, as it gave her a chance to think through her years of ministry and realize how the Lord Almighty has been faithful and dependable in all her years of service to Him.

Christine Phumelele Xaba has supported her husband in ministry for 44 years—first as he served in the pastorate and later as a lecturer and principal of the Union Bible Institute. Mrs. Xaba trained as a nurse at Raleigh Fitkin Memorial Hospital in Swaziland and worked in that profession until retirement. She is also a graduate of the Union Bible Institute where she taught for a short while. She has three grown children. Mrs. Xaba has been looking for a book for pastors' wives since she married her husband. As they pastored churches in KwaZulu-Natal early in their marriage, she encountered many situations in which she didn't know what to do. She learned through her own experience and mistakes, and is thankful for the chance to share these lessons with others.

Endnotes

Chapter 1

1. Adapted from Leah Marasigan Darwin, *Yes! I'm a Pastor's Wife! 2nd edition*, (Makati City, Philippines: Church Strengthening Ministry, Inc., 2007), 26.
2. Quoted by Ruth Meyers and Warren Myers, in *Thirty-one Days of Praise*, (Multnomah, Oregon: Multnomah Publishers, 1994), 97.

Chapter 2

1. Larry Crabb, *Inside Out* (Colorado Springs, Colorado: Navpress, 1988).
2. Some of the ideas from this section are taken from Leah Marasigan Darwin, *Yes! I'm a Pastor's Wife! 2nd edition* (Makati City, Philippines: Church Strengthening Ministry, Inc., 2007), Chapter 2.
3. John MacArthur, *The MacArthur Study Bible* (Nashville, Tennessee: Word Publishing, a division of Thomas Nelson, Inc., 1997), 1717.

Chapter 4

1. An excellent resource on a woman's priorities is Elizabeth George, *A Woman After God's Own Heart*, (Eugene, Oregon: Harvest House, 1997). See also Leah Marasigan Darwin, *Yes! I'm a Pastor's Wife! 2nd edition*, (Makati City, Philippines: Church Strengthening Ministry, Inc., 2007), Chapter 4.
2. UBI Publishing has available two daily devotional guides in isiZulu, *Incazelo Yezwi Lemihla Ngemihla, Incwadi Yokuqala neYesibili*, by B.A. Johanson.
3. William Wordsworth, "The World is Too Much with Us".
4. John W. Peterson, "It's Not an Easy Road".

Chapter 5

1. Water Trobisch, *I Married You* (Bolivar, Missouri: Quiet Waters Publications, 2000), 29.
2. Leah Marasigan Darwin, *Yes! I'm a Pastor's Wife! 2nd edition* (Makati City, Philippines: Church Strengthening Ministry, Inc., 2007), Chapters 5

and 6.
3   Linda Dillow, *Creative Counnterpart* (Nashville, TN: Thomas Nelson, 1977).
4   Shaunti Feldhahn, *For Women Only* (Sisters, Oregon: Multnomah Publishers, 2004), 67.
5   Feldhahn, 23.
6   James Dobson, *What wives wish their husbands knew about women* (Wheaton, Illinois: Tyndale House Publishers, 1975), 119.
7   Agrippa Goodman Khathide, *Bone of my Bones* (Johannesburg, South Africa: AcadSA, 2007), 107.
8   Grace Kimathi, *Courting in Marriage,* (Nairobi, Kenya: Uzima Press, 2003), 77.
9   Trobisch, 68.

Chapter 6

1   Elizabeth George, *A Woman After God's Own Heart*, (Eugene, Oregon: Harvest House, 1997), 98.
2   Stormie Omartian, *The Power of a Praying Parent* (Eugene, Oregon: Harvest House Publishers, 2007).
3   UBI Publishing has produced a family devotional guide in isiZulu, *Masifundisane Ngezaphezulu.*, by Dumisile Gumede and Ruth Hall.
4   One good resource is Bruce Narramore's book, *Parenting With Love and Limits* (Grand Rapids, Michigan: Zondervan Publishing House, 1979).
5   Some of these ideas to help your "PK's", and more, can be found in the following articles: Lisa Whittle, "Ministry Kids Have Needs, Too!" www.justbetweenus.org, accessed 10 June, 2010, and "9 Ways You Can Help Your Kids" www.justbetweenus.org, accessed 10 June, 2010.

Chapter 7

1   Karen Burton Mains, *Open Heart, Open Home* (Elgin, Illinois: David C. Cook Publishing Co., 1976).

Chapter 8

1   Adapted from George W. Trimble, *The Gift of Giving* (Salt River: The Methodist Church of Southern Africa and the Methodist Publishing House, 2003), 7.

2. Caroline Adalla, *Stewardship: Challenging the Church in Africa* (Florida, South Africa: Africa Nazarene Publications, 2002), 64.
3. Adapted from Adalla, 66-69.
4. Adalla, 76-78.
5. Trimble, 64.
6. Klaus Nürnberger, *Making Ends Meet* (Pietermaritzburg: Cluster Publications, and Pretoria: The C B Powell Centre, 2008), 36.
7. Trimble, 64-66.
8. The following principles about debt are summarised from Chapter 11 of Trimble's book, *The Gift of Giving*, 67-71. Used with permission.
9. Leah Marasigan Darwin, *Yes! I'm a Pastor's Wife! 2nd edition* (Makati City, Philippines: Church Strengthening Ministry, Inc., 2007), 165.
10. Trimble, 22.
11. Adalla, 60.

Chapter 10

1. Ken Sande, *The Peacemaker* (Grand Rapids, Michigan: Baker Books, 1997), 24. This section on a biblical view of conflict, as well as the sections on confession, forgiveness, and consequences, is based largely on this excellent resource.
2. Leah Marasigan Darwin, *Yes! I'm a Pastor's Wife! 2nd edition* (Makati City, Philippines: Church Strengthening Ministry, Inc., 2007), 134.
3. B. A. Johanson, *Isifundiso Sebhayibheli* (Hilton, South Africa: Union Bible Institute), 308.
4. Darwin, 134.
5. Dale Carnegie, *How to Stop Worrying and Start Living* (New York: Simon and Schuster, 1984), 201.
6. Carnegie, 203.
7. Darwin, 145.
8. H. Norman Wright, *So You're Getting Married* (Ventura, CA: Regal Books, 1985), 243.
9. Sande, 188.
10. Fran and Les Hewitt, *The Power of Focus for Women* (Deerfield Beach, FL: Health Communications, Inc., 2003), 196.
11. Sande, 188-190.
12. Sande, 198.
13. Hewitt, 200.

14 Notes from a retreat by Eagles' Cove Ministries.
15 Sande, 197.
16 T.D. Jakes, *The Lady, Her Lover and Her Lord* ((New York: Berkley Books, 1998).

Chapter 11

1. Gary R. Collins, *Christian Counseling: A Comprehensive Guide*, third edition (Thomas Nelson Publishers, 2007), 17-18.
2. See *Choosing Hope*, (Bukuru, Nigeria: African Chrsitian Textbooks, 2003), 60-61, and Collins, 64-67.
3. See *Choosing Hope*, (Bukuru, Nigeria: African Chrsitian Textbooks, 2003), 61-62 and Glen Slabber, *Christian Care Training: Volume 3, Module 18*.
4. Christian Listeners-KZN, *Learning to Listen: A Five Session Mini-course* (Acorn Christian Foundation, 2000)
5. Slabber, *Modules 20 and 23*.
6. Slabber, *Module 23*.
7. Adapted from Christian Listeners-KZN, 4.

Chapter 13

1. This discussion of the Biblical principles and benefits of a sabbath rest is summarised from Lynne Baab's book, *Sabbath Keeping: Finding Freedom in the Rhythms of Rest* (Downers Grove, Illinois: Intervarsity Press, 2005). We recommend this book for further study on this topic.
2. Adapted from Lynne Baab's questions in her book, *Sabbath Keeping*.

Appendix 2

1. This information is summarised and adapted from *The Church in an HIV+ World: A Practical Handbook,* Daniela Gennrich, editor, (Pietermaritzburg, South Africa: Cluster Publications, 2004), 143-145.